P9-CRW-279

drop~dead
easy knits

drop~dead easy knits

GALE ZUCKER,
MARY LOU EGAN,
AND KIRSTEN KAPUR

CLARKSON POTTER / PUBLISHERS
New York

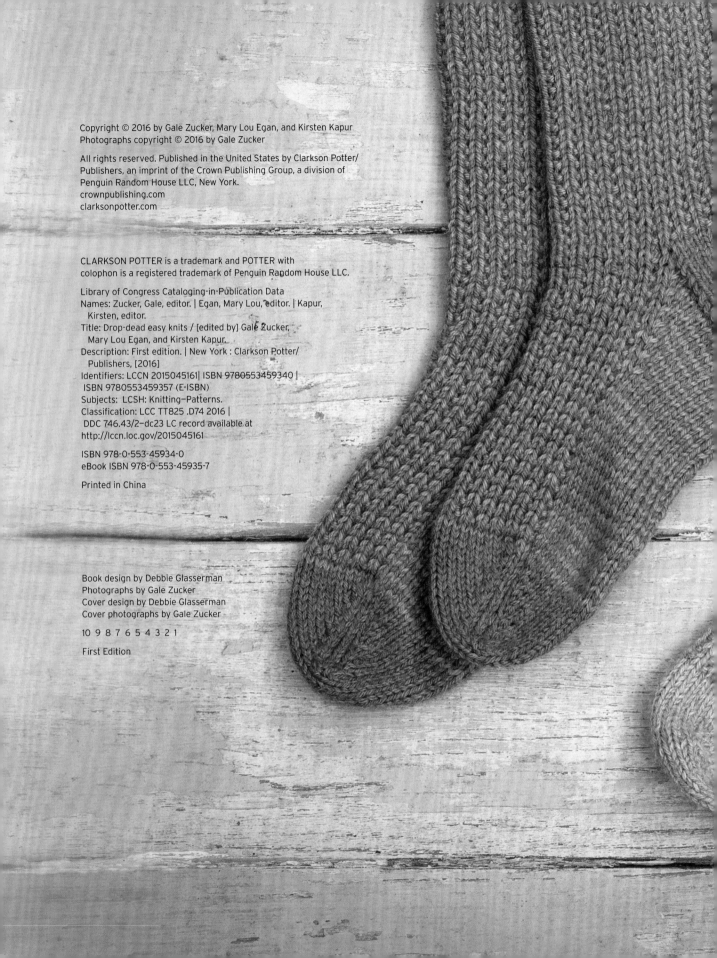

Copyright © 2016 by Gale Zucker, Mary Lou Egan, and Kirsten Kapur
Photographs copyright © 2016 by Gale Zucker

All rights reserved. Published in the United States by Clarkson Potter/
Publishers, an imprint of the Crown Publishing Group, a division of
Penguin Random House LLC, New York.
crownpublishing.com
clarksonpotter.com

CLARKSON POTTER is a trademark and POTTER with
colophon is a registered trademark of Penguin Random House LLC.

Library of Congress Cataloging-in-Publication Data
Names: Zucker, Gale, editor. | Egan, Mary Lou, editor. | Kapur,
    Kirsten, editor.
Title: Drop-dead easy knits / [edited by] Gale Zucker,
    Mary Lou Egan, and Kirsten Kapur.
Description: First edition. | New York : Clarkson Potter/
    Publishers, [2016]
Identifiers: LCCN 2015045161| ISBN 9780553459340 |
 ISBN 9780553459357 (E-ISBN)
Subjects: LCSH: Knitting—Patterns.
Classification: LCC TT825 .D74 2016 |
    DDC 746.43/2—dc23 LC record available at
http://lccn.loc.gov/2015045161

ISBN 978-0-553-45934-0
eBook ISBN 978-0-553-45935-7

Printed in China

Book design by Debbie Glasserman
Photographs by Gale Zucker
Cover design by Debbie Glasserman
Cover photographs by Gale Zucker

10 9 8 7 6 5 4 3 2 1

First Edition

For Guy, who has kept the home fires burning while I burned the midnight oil. MLE

To Kiran, Anders, Isabella, and Sofia, creative spirits, supporters of dreams, and the four who know how to challenge me in the best ways possible. xoxo KAGK

For Rita and for Zoe, with love—two creative and intrepid spirits I'm blessed to have in my life. xo GZ

CONTENTS

INTRODUCTION

WHENEVER THE THREE OF US GET TOGETHER, MARY LOU invariably has something wonderful on her needles. In admiration, we ask what she's knitting, and the answer is inevitably, "Oh . . . this? It's *easy*. No, really, I know it doesn't look it, *but it's drop-dead easy.*"

And, of course, as soon as she says those words, we're scrambling to acquire the pattern and cast on. It's become something of a running joke. Despite our advanced knitting skills and projects aplenty in progress, we *cannot resist* a wonderful, stylish pattern that is drop-dead easy.

For the three of us—Mary Lou, Kirsten, and Gale—knitting is part of both our professional lives and the way we live. Wherever we are, knitting is what we do in between more demanding tasks, to relax, to help us think, to comfort us, to endure the waits and annoyances of modern society, and to enhance our leisure time.

Put on hold for twenty minutes with tech support? Try knitting. Waiting to have your driver's license renewed? So much less painful when adding a couple of inches onto a sock. Relaxing on the porch with friends and a bottle of wine? There's no reason why you shouldn't be working on a knitting project at the same time.

All of which is to say that we three are just like you. We want what you want: projects that look gorgeous but are drop-dead easy to make.

The three of us were knitting around a campfire in Maine—the sort of scenario we envision for our chapter "Drinking Buddies"—

when we came up with the idea for this book. Over wine and lobsters, we talked about projects we like: smart patterns with long stretches where you can go on automatic pilot between the elements that require focus. We realized that if we combined our strengths as three lifelong knitters, we could stew up a delicious collection of patterns ourselves. Kirsten's glorious abilities with color, lace, and shaping create designs *that are addictive to knit.* Mary Lou is a wise and patient knitting teacher with a wicked sense of humor, all of which she channels into modern classic knits. Gale's passion for visual storytelling as a professional commercial photographer stylishly captures the look and feel of these patterns with all the understanding of a passionate knitter. Together we had the ingredients to create an arsenal of knitting projects that would satisfy a knitter's soul but wouldn't require *complete* concentration.

Over the next few months, we spent a lot of time thinking about the kinds of patterns we most want and where we want to knit them. In some situations—travel, for instance—we choose projects that are portable. They should engage us enough to pass the time, but we should be able to put them down and pick them up painlessly, and as often as needed. These are the kinds of designs we include in "The Waiting Game."

We like to work a big, heavy wrap on a chilly winter afternoon, the kind we offer in "Cold Hands, Warm Hearts." We want knits both to give as gifts to our families and to get us through gatherings with our relatives, when togetherness frays our edges—patterns for these scenarios can be found in "Family Entanglements." When we're away with friends for the weekend, we want patterns that you can chat your way through at knit night without needing to rip out the next day, or knit with friends as pieces, then join to make a beautiful whole. You, too? You'll find some in our "Drinking Buddies" chapter.

We like baby designs that are adorable but not fussy to make and to wear, and that's just what we created in "Bursting with Joy." We want projects to pull us through the minutes when we're waiting around at conferences, on the subway, and in medical clinics. These portable projects can be found in "The Waiting Game." Lastly, we adore knitting at the beach, where alternatives to woolly fibers are the next best thing to a margarita and a chair in the sand. So, we have gorgeous designs in linen, silk, and cotton in "No Sheep at the Shore."

And we love designs that are yarn-store friendly, so we can pop in to our favorite local yarn shop and have the immediate gratification of plucking the suggested skeins off the shelf.

Though patterns like these are in demand, we know it's hard to find a well-designed, chic collection that keeps our minds free and our hands busy. To maximize both the carefree and the detailed aspects of each piece, we've highlighted sections where you can knit away on "cruise control," and "concentration zones" where you will need to focus. We've also rated each project for attention needed, so you can plan your relaxation knitting accordingly (for difficulty ratings, please turn to page 137).

We enjoyed every minute of brainstorming and designing and test knitting, as well as producing our photos to show the knits in action on our beautiful models. We've grouped them by situations we find ourselves in when we call on our knitting to relax, entertain, or soothe us.

What are you waiting for? Cast on!

cold hands, warm hearts

IS ANYTHING MORE CONVENIENT THAN A COZY PROJECT at a cold-weather sports practice, ice skating rink, or a cabin in the mountains? Knitting with warm fluffy fibers—wool, alpaca, and blends—is what we do when the thermometer dips. The five projects in this chapter will keep your fingers toasty and happy while you knit them and make comfy wardrobe additions once completed.

Whether you are in the mood for creating—and snuggling into—the glamorous Glama Wrap, the quick finish of the Portillo Cowl, the cozy rhythm of the Oxbo Socks, the elegantly functional Turoa Mitts, or the must-have-will-never-take-off Camurac Cardigan, we assure you that all are (mostly) drop-dead easy *and* will keep you from chilling to the bone.

CAMURAC CARDIGAN

design by kirsten kapur

We all have those items in our wardrobe that go easily from office to home, from park to party—the ones we wear so often our friends have started to notice. The Camurac Cardigan is one of those pieces. It will keep you snuggly warm on the coldest days of winter, or make the perfect sweater jacket for in-between autumn temperatures. Worked in pieces in Aran-weight yarn, the Camurac Cardigan is a quick knit that you can take along for a weekend at the cabin or on your commute.

DIFFICULTY LEVEL
Relaxed

SIZES
XS (S, M, L, 1X, 2X)
Shown in size S

FINISHED MEASUREMENTS
Bust: 34½ (39, 42, 45½, 50, 54½)"
(87.5 [99, 106.5, 115.5, 127, 138]cm) with
4" (10cm) overlap at front edge

MATERIALS
7 (7, 8, 8, 9, 10) skeins Quince & Co.
Osprey, 100% American wool, 3½ oz
(100g), 170 yd (155m), in 101 Egret

1 pair US size 10 (6mm) straight needles
(adjust needle size as necessary to
obtain gauge)
1 US size 10 (6mm) 40" (100cm) circular
needle (adjust size as necessary to
obtain gauge). Although this project is
worked flat, a circular needle is used
when working the front bands, to hold
the large number of stitches.
Stitch holder or scrap yarn
Tapestry needle

GAUGE AFTER BLOCKING
15 stitches and 22 rows = 4" (10cm) in
stockinette stitch

STITCH PATTERN
Textured Rib Pattern
Multiple of 3 stitches, plus 2.
Row 1 (RS): *K2, p1; repeat from * to
last 2 stitches, k2.
Row 2 (WS): *P2, k1; repeat from * to
last 2 stitches, p2.
Row 3: Repeat row 1.
Row 4: Knit.
Repeat rows 1-4 for pattern.

PATTERN INSTRUCTIONS

BACK

Cast on 67 (75, 83, 91, 97, 105) stitches.

Row 1 (RS): *k1 tbl, p1; repeat from * to last stitch, k1 tbl.

Row 2 (WS): *P1 tbl, k1; repeat from * to last stitch, p1 tbl.

Work rows 1 and 2 three more times, for a total of 4 times (8 rows total). Work even in stockinette stitch until body measures 19 (19, 18¾, 18½, 18¼, 18)" (48.5 [48.5, 47.5, 47, 46.5, 45.5]cm) from the cast-on edge. End with a wrong-side row, ready to begin a right-side row.

ARMHOLES

Continue working in stockinette stitch while binding off 5 (6, 7, 8, 9, 11) stitches at the beginning of the next 2 rows—57 (63, 69, 75, 79, 83) stitches.

Armhole Decrease

Row 1 (decrease) (RS): K1, ssk, knit to last 3 stitches, k2tog, k1.

Row 2 (WS): Purl.

Work rows 1 and 2 above 4 (5, 6, 7, 8, 10) more times, for a total of 5 (6, 7, 8, 9, 11) times—47 (51, 55, 59, 61, 61) stitches.

Continue to work in stockinette stitch until armhole measures 6½ (7, 7½, 8, 8½, 9)" (16.5 [18, 19, 20.5, 21.5, 23]cm). End with a wrong-side row, ready to begin a right-side row.

SHAPE BACK NECK

Knit the first 13 (15, 17, 18, 19, 19) stitches. Place these stitches on a holder or a piece of scrap yarn. Bind off the next 21 (21, 21, 23, 23, 23) stitches. Knit to end—13 (15, 17, 18, 19, 19) stitches.

SHAPE LEFT SHOULDER

Row 1 (WS): Purl.

Row 2 (decrease) (RS): K1, ssk, k6 (7, 8, 8, 9, 9), wrap the next stitch and turn—12 (14, 16, 17, 18, 18) stitches.

Row 3: Purl.

Row 4 (decrease): K1, ssk, k1 (1, 1, 1, 2, 2), wrap the next stitch and turn—11 (13, 15, 16, 17, 17) stitches.

Row 5: Purl.

Row 6 (decrease): K1, ssk, knit to end, picking up the wraps as you encounter them and knitting them together with the stitch that they wrap—10 (12, 14, 15, 16, 16) stitches. Bind off.

RIGHT SHOULDER

Place the 13 (15, 17, 18, 19, 19) held stitches back on the needles. Rejoin the yarn at the neck edge.

Row 1 (WS): Purl.

Row 2 (decrease) (RS): Knit to the last 3 stitches, k2tog, k1—12 (14, 16, 17, 18, 18) stitches.

Row 3: P8 (9, 10, 10, 11, 11), wrap the next stitch and turn.

Row 4 (decrease): Knit to the last 3 stitches, k2tog, k1—11 (13, 15, 16, 17, 17) stitches.

Row 5: P3 (3, 3, 3, 4, 4), wrap the next stitch and turn.

Row 6 (decrease): K0 (0, 0, 0, 1, 1), k2tog, k1—10 (12, 14, 15, 16, 16) stitches.

Row 7: Purl, picking up the wraps as you come to them and purling them together with the stitch they wrap. Bind off.

LEFT FRONT

Cast on 27 (31, 33, 37, 41, 45) stitches.

Work as for Back until piece measures 17 (17, 16¾, 16½, 16¼, 16)" (43 [43, 42.5, 42, 41, 40.5]cm) from cast-on edge, ending with a wrong-side row, ready to begin a right-side row.

⚠ CONCENTRATION ZONE

Note: *Read ahead! Neckline and armhole shaping are worked at the same time.*

SHAPE NECKLINE

Decrease row (RS): Knit to the last 3 stitches, k2tog, k1.

Work 3 (5, 7, 7, 5, 5) rows in stockinette stitch.

Repeat these 4 (6, 8, 8, 6, 6) rows 6 (6, 4, 5, 6, 6) more times, for a total of 7 (7, 5, 6, 7, 7) times.

At the same time, when work measures 19 (19, 18¾, 18½, 18¼, 18)" (48.5 [48.5, 47.5, 47, 46.5, 45.5] cm), ending with a wrong-side row and ready to begin a right-side row, shape armhole as follows:

Row 1 (RS): Bind off 5 (6, 7, 8, 9, 11) stitches, work as established to end.

Row 2 (WS): Purl.

ARMHOLE DECREASES

Row 1 (decrease) (RS): K1, ssk, work as established to end.

Row 2 (WS): Purl.

Work rows 1 and 2 above 4 (5, 6, 7, 8, 10) more times, for a total of 5 (6, 7, 8, 9, 11) times.

When all neckline and armhole decreases have been worked, 10 (12, 14, 15, 16, 16) stitches remain.

🕹 CRUISE CONTROL

Continue to work in stockinette stitch until armhole measures 6½ (7, 7½, 8, 8½, 9)" (16.5 [18, 19, 20.5, 21.5, 23]cm). End with a right-side row, ready to begin a wrong-side row.

SHAPE LEFT SHOULDER

Row 1 (WS): Purl.

Row 2 (RS): Knit.

Row 3: P6 (7, 8, 8, 9, 9), wrap the next stitch and turn.
Row 4: Knit.
Row 5: P2 (2, 2, 2, 3, 3), wrap the next stitch and turn.
Row 6: Knit.
Row 7: Purl, picking up the wraps as you come to them and purling them together with the stitch they wrap. Bind off.

LEFT FRONT POCKET

With the right side facing, pick up and knit 27 (31, 33, 37, 41, 45) stitches, 1 in each of the stitches in the row just above the bottom ribbing.
Row 1 (RS): K1 (3, 1, 3, 2, 1), *p1, k2; repeat from * to last 2 (4, 2, 4, 3, 2) stitches, p1, k1 (3, 1, 3, 2, 1).
Row 2 (WS): P1 (3, 1, 3, 2, 1), *k1, p2; repeat from * to last 2 (4, 2, 4, 3, 2) stitches, k1, p1 (3, 1, 3, 2, 1).
Row 3: Repeat row 1.
Row 4: P1, knit to last stitch, p1.
Work rows 1–4 five more times, for a total of 6 times. Work rows 1–3 once more.

RIBBING

Row 1 (WS): P1 *k1, p1 tbl; repeat from * to last 2 stitches, k1, p1.
Row 2 (RS): K1, *p1, k1 tbl; repeat from * to last 2 stitches, p1, k1.

Work rows 1 and 2 once more, for a total of 2 times.
Bind off.

RIGHT FRONT

Cast on 27 (31, 33, 37, 41, 45) stitches.
Work as for Back until piece measures 17 (17, 16¾, 16½, 16¼, 16)" (43 [43, 42.5, 42, 41, 40.5]cm) from cast-on edge, ending with a wrong-side row and ready to begin a right-side row.

⚠ CONCENTRATION ZONE

Note: Read ahead! Neckline and armhole shaping are worked at the same time.

SHAPE NECKLINE

Decrease Row (RS): K1, ssk, knit to end.
Work 3 (5, 7, 7, 5, 5) rows in stockinette stitch.
Repeat these 4 (6, 8, 8, 6, 6) rows 6 (6, 4, 5, 6, 6) more times, for a total of 7 (7, 5, 6, 7, 7) times.
At the same time, when work measures 19 (19, 18¾, 18½, 18¼, 18)" (48.5 [48.5, 47.5, 47, 46.5, 45.5] cm), ending with a right-side row, shape armhole as follows:

Next Row (WS): Bind off 5 (6, 7, 8, 9, 11) stitches, work as established to end.

ARMHOLE DECREASES

Row 1 (decrease) (RS): Work as established to last 3 stitches, k2tog, k1.
Row 2 (WS): Purl.
Work rows 1 and 2 above 4 (5, 6, 7, 8, 10) more times, for a total of 5 (6, 7, 8, 9, 11) times.
When all neckline and armhole decreases have been worked, 10 (12, 14, 15, 16, 16) stitches remain.

🕹 CRUISE CONTROL

Continue to work in stockinette stitch until armhole measures 6½ (7, 7½, 8, 8½, 9)" (16.5 [18, 19, 20.5, 21.5, 23]cm). End with a right-side row, ready to begin a wrong-side row.

SHAPE RIGHT SHOULDER

Row 1 (WS): Purl.
Row 2 (RS): K6 (7, 8, 8, 9, 9), wrap the next stitch and turn.
Row 3: Purl.
Row 4: K2 (2, 2, 2, 3, 3), wrap the next stitch and turn.
Row 5: Purl.

Row 6: Knit, picking up the wraps as you come to them and knitting them together with the stitch that they wrap.
Bind off.

RIGHT FRONT POCKET
Work as for Left Front Pocket.

SLEEVES (MAKE 2)
Cast on 38 (38, 40, 44, 46, 48) stitches.
Row 1 (RS): *K1 tbl, p1; repeat from * to end.
Row 2 (WS): *K1, p1 tbl; repeat from * to end.
Work rows 1 and 2 three more times, for a total of 4 times (8 rows total).
Work 2 rows in stockinette stitch, starting with a knit row.
Increase row (RS): K2, M1R, knit to 2 stitches from end, M1L, k2.
Work 21 (17, 17, 17, 11, 7) rows in stockinette stitch as established.
Work the 22 (18, 18, 18, 12, 8) rows above 2 (3, 3, 3, 5, 8) more times, for a total of 3 (4, 4, 4, 6, 9) times—44 (46, 48, 52, 58, 66) stitches.
Work in stockinette stitch until sleeve measures 16½ (17, 17, 17½, 17½, 18)" (42 [43, 43, 44.5, 44.5, 45.5]cm) from cast-on edge. End with a wrong-side row, ready to begin a right-side row.

Sleeve Cap
Continue working in stockinette stitch while binding off 5 (6, 7, 8, 9, 11) stitches at the beginning of the next 2 rows—34 (34, 34, 36, 40 44) stitches.

Sleeve Cap Decreases
Row 1 decrease (RS): K1, ssk, knit to last 3 stitches, k2tog, k1.
Row 2 (WS): Purl.
Work rows 1 and 2 above 4 (5, 6, 7, 8, 10) more times, for a total of 5 (6, 7, 8, 9, 11) times—24 (22, 20, 20, 22, 22) stitches.
Work in stockinette stitch for 16 (18, 20, 20, 20, 18) rows. End with a wrong-side row, ready to begin a right-side row.

Shape Top of Sleeve Cap
Row 1 (decrease) (RS): K1, ssk, knit to last 3 stitches, k2tog, k1.
Row 2 (decrease) (WS): P1, p2tog tbl, purl to the last 3 stitches, p2tog, p1.
Work rows 1 and 2 above 3 (2, 2, 2, 2, 2) more times, for a total of 4 (3, 3, 3, 3, 3) times.
Bind off the remaining 8 (10, 8, 8, 10, 10) stitches.

FINISHING
Sew Front pieces to Back at shoulders.
Sew side seams, sewing the side edge of the pockets into the side seam as you get to them.
Sew sleeve caps into armholes, easing as necessary to fit.

Front and Neck Band
With the right side facing and using the circular needle, pick up and knit 104 (107, 107, 109, 109, 112) stitches along the Right Front edge, picking up and knitting through the pocket as well as the front piece as you get to it.
Continuing along the Back neck, pick up and knit 28 (28, 28, 30, 30, 30) stitches.
Continuing down the Left Front edge, pick up and knit 104 (107, 107, 109, 109, 112) stitches, picking up and knitting through the pocket as well as the front piece as you get to it—236 (242, 242, 248, 248, 254) stitches.
Row 1 (WS): P2, *k1, p2; repeat from * to end.
Row 2 (RS): K2, *p1, k2; repeat from * to end.
Row 3: Knit.
Row 4: Repeat row 2.
Work rows 1-4 four more times, for a total of 5 times.
Work rows 1 and 2 once more.
Bind off.
Weave in all ends.
Block to measurements in schematic.

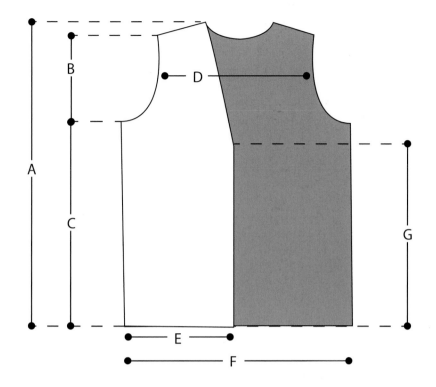

A: 26½ (27, 27¼, 27½, 27¾, 28)" (67.5 [68.5, 69, 70, 70.5, 71]cm)
B: 6½ (7, 7½, 8, 8½, 9)" (16.5 [18, 19, 20.5, 21.5, 23]cm)
C: 19 (19, 18¾, 18½, 18¼, 18)" (48.5 [48.5, 47.5, 47, 46.5, 45.5]cm)
D: 12½ (13½, 14½, 15¾, 16¼, 16¼)" (32 [34.5, 37, 40, 41, 41]cm)
E: 10½ (11¾, 12¼, 13¼, 14½, 15½)" (26.5 [30, 31, 33.5, 37, 39.5]cm)
F: 17¼ (19½, 21½, 23¾, 25¼, 27½)" (44 [49.5, 54.5, 60.5, 64, 70]cm)
G: 17 (17, 16¾, 16½, 16¼, 16)" (43 [43, 42.5, 42, 41, 40.5]cm)

SLEEVE
H: 16½ (17, 17, 17½, 17½, 18)" (42 [43, 43, 44.5, 44.5, 45.5]cm)
I: 11¼ (11¾, 12¼, 13¼, 15, 17)" (28.5 [30, 31, 33.5, 38, 43]cm)
J: 9½ (9½, 10, 11¼, 11¾, 12¼)" (24 [24, 25.5, 28.5, 30, 31]cm)

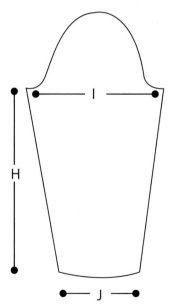

GLAMA WRAP

design by kirsten kapur

W e love nothing more than knitting a warm shawl by the fire on a cold night. As the Glama Wrap grows, you can spread the finished end across your lap to keep you extra toasty. Worked in bulky yarn with a simple stitch pattern, this cozy wrap knits up so quickly you'll find yourself wanting to cast on another one as soon as you finish the first.

DIFFICULTY LEVEL
Relaxed

SIZES
Scarf, (Wrap)
(Shown as wrap)

FINISHED MEASUREMENTS
Width: 10 (23½)" (25.5 [59.5]cm)
Length: 67 (67)" (170 [170]cm)

MATERIALS
4 (8) skeins Malabrigo Mecha, 100% superwash merino, 3½ oz (100g), 130 yd (120m), in Polar Morn

1 US size 11 (8mm) 24 (32)" (60 [80]cm) circular needle (adjust needle size as necessary to obtain gauge)
2 stitch markers
Tapestry needle

GAUGE AFTER BLOCKING
13 stitches and 21 rows = 4" (10cm) in stockinette stitch
3 multiples of dropped stitch pattern = 4" (10cm) wide
1 repeat of dropped stitch pattern = 4" (10cm) high

SPECIAL STITCH
Drop stitch: **Slip the stitch off the needle and let it unravel to the yarn over 8 rows below.**

STITCH PATTERN
Dropped Stitch Pattern
  Multiple of 4 stitches, plus 2. See note below.
  Note: This stitch pattern changes stitch counts throughout. For swatching purposes, cast on a multiple of 4 plus 2 stitches. Work the setup row once only.
Setup row (RS): *K1, yo, k1, p2; work from * to last 2 stitches, k1, yo, k1.
Row 1 (WS): P3, *k2, p3; work from * to end.
Row 2: *K3, p2; work from * to last 3 stitches, k3.
Rows 3-6: Repeat rows 1 and 2.
Row 7: Repeat row 1.
Row 8: *K1, drop stitch, k1, p1, yo, p1; work from * to last 3 stitches, k1, drop stitch, k1.
Row 9: P2, *k3, p2; work from * to end.
Row 10: *K2, p3; work from * to last 2 stitches, k2.
Rows 11-14: Repeat rows 9 and 10.
Row 15: Repeat row 9.
Row 16: *K1, yo, k1, p2, drop stitch, p1; work from * to last 2 stitches, k1, yo, k1.
Repeat rows 1-16 for pattern.

PATTERN INSTRUCTIONS

Cast on 30 (70) stitches.

Work in garter stitch for 10 rows.

Setup row (RS): K2, place marker, *k1, yo, k1, p2; work from * 5 (15) more times for a total of 6 (16) times, k1, yo, k1, place marker, k2–37 (87) stitches.

Row 1 (WS): K2, p3, *k2, p3; work from * 5 (15) more times for a total of 6 (16) times, k2.

Row 2 (RS): K2, *k3, p2; work from * 5 (15) more times, for a total of 6 (16) times, k5.

Rows 3–6: Repeat rows 1 and 2.

Row 7: Repeat row 1.

Row 8: K2, *k1, drop stitch, k1, p1, yo, p1; work from * 5 (15) more times for a total of 6 (16) times, k1, drop stitch, k3–36 (86) stitches.

Row 9 (WS): K2, p2, *k3, p2; work from * 5 (15) more times, for a total of 6 (16) times, k2.

Row 10 (RS): K2, *k2, p3; work from * 5 (15) more times, for a total of 6 (16) times, k4.

Rows 11–14: Repeat rows 9 and 10 twice.

Row 15: Repeat row 9.

Row 16: K2, *k1, yo, k1, p1, drop stitch, p1; work from * 5 (15) more times, for a total of 6 (16) times, k1, yo, k3–37 (87) stitches.

Repeat rows 1–16 for pattern.

Continue to work the first 2 and the last 2 stitches in garter stitch while working the dropped stitch pattern between the markers. Work rows 1–16 a total of 16 times.

Work rows 1–7 once more.

Next row: K2, *k1, drop stitch, k1, p2; work from * 5 (15) more times, for a total of 6 (16) times, k1, drop stitch, k3–30 (70) stitches.

Work 10 rows in garter stitch.

Bind off.

FINISHING

Weave in ends.

Block.

PORTILLO COWL

design by gale zucker

Some knitting projects require hours of finishing, meticulous blocking, multiple ends woven in, and carefully matched and sewn pieces. On the other end of the spectrum you'll find the Portillo Cowl. This cushy, bulky, quick-to-knit and easy-to-wear cowl uses two colors of yarn. Knit in basic garter stitch in the round, a graphically pleasing fabric appears with no effort at all. Use a kettle-dyed Malabrigo Rasta as we did, and the design is elevated beyond the basic knit that it is. Got fear of finishing? This one's for you (also see the Grand Central Scarf on page 51).

DIFFICULTY LEVEL
Mindless

SIZE
One size

FINISHED MEASUREMENTS
Circumference: 51" (129.5cm)
Depth: 6" (15cm)

MATERIALS
Malabrigo Rasta, 100% merino wool, 5¼ oz (150g), 90 yd (82m).

MC: 1 skein in Plomo; CC: 1 skein in Natural.

1 US size 15 (10mm) 40" (100cm) circular needle (adjust needle size as necessary to obtain gauge)
Stitch marker
1 US size M/N-13 (9mm) crochet hook for weaving in ends

GAUGE AFTER BLOCKING
5½ stitches and 17 rows = 4" (10cm) in garter stitch

PATTERN NOTES
This cowl is worked in one piece, in the round.
When alternating colors in the stripes, yarns may be carried up on the wrong side of the work.
A crochet hook is used to weave in the ends because of the thickness of the yarn.
This cowl uses all but a few yards of the MC. Work your swatch in the CC. If your gauge differs from that specified or if you increase the size, extra yarn may be needed.

PATTERN INSTRUCTIONS

With MC, cast on 70 stitches.
Note: *It is important to keep the cast-on loose. Take care to space the cast-on stitches out over the needle as you form them.*
Join to work in the round, being careful not to twist the stitches. Place stitch marker for the beginning of the round.
Setup round: With CC, purl.
Round 1: With MC, knit.
Round 2: With CC, purl.
Work rounds 1 and 2 above 7 more times, for a total of 8 times.
Cut CC, leaving a tail long enough to weave in.
Continue working with MC only.
Round 1: Knit.
Round 2: Purl.
Work rounds 1 and 2 above twice more, for a total of 3 times.
Work round 1 once more.
Rejoin CC and purl 1 round.
Cut CC, leaving a tail long enough to weave in.
Bind off very loosely with MC as follows: K1, transfer the stitch just knit back onto the left needle, *k2tog through the back loop, transfer the stitch just knit purlwise back onto the left needle; repeat from * until all stitches are bound off.
Pull the yarn through the remaining stitch to secure.
Cut the yarn, leaving a tail long enough to weave in.

FINISHING
Weave in all ends, using the crochet hook to pull the tail through the stitches on the inside of the work.
Block.

TUROA MITTS

design by kirsten kapur

Winter activities often require accessories that keep hands warm and fingers free. The pieces we love can be worn in our drafty home office, while playing guitar at a bonfire, or when walking the dog in the early morning—not to mention sitting in football bleachers. The pretty Turoa Mitts, worked in sportweight yarn, are just right for these occasions. Worked in the round, the delicate cables give the Turoa an elegant look without sacrificing their practicality.

DIFFICULTY LEVEL
Relaxed

SIZES
S (M, L)

FINISHED MEASUREMENTS
Circumference: 6 (6¾, 7½)" (15 [17, 19]cm)
Length: 11 (11½, 12)" (26.5 [28, 29]cm)

MATERIALS
Green mitts: 2 (2, 2) skeins The Fibre Company Road to China Light, 65% baby alpaca, 15% silk, 10% camel, 10% cashmere, 1¾ oz (50g), 159 yd (145.5m), in Abalone

Yellow mitts: 1 (1, 1) skein Anzula Oasis, 70% silk, 30% camel, 4 oz (114g), 375 yd (343m), in Temperance

1 set of 5 US size 4 (3.5mm) double-pointed needles (adjust needle size as necessary to obtain gauge)
3 stitch markers
Cable needle
Scrap yarn
Tapestry needle

GAUGE AFTER BLOCKING
24 stitches and 38 rows = 4" (10cm) in stockinette stitch

SPECIAL STITCHES
1 over 2 LC: Place the next stitch on a cable needle and hold in front. K2, k1 from the cable needle.
1 over 2 RC: Place the next 2 stitches on a cable needle and hold in back. K1, k2 from the cable needle.

STITCH PATTERN
Cable Pattern
Multiple of 7 stitches, plus 1.
Rounds 1 and 2: *P1, k6; work from * twice more for a total of 3 times, p1.
Rounds 3 and 4: *P1, slip 1, k4, slip 1; work from * twice more for a total of 3 times, p1.
Round 5: *P1, *1 over 2 LC*, *1 over 2 RC*; work from * 3 times, p1.

PATTERN INSTRUCTIONS

CUFF

Cast on 44 (48, 52) stitches.

Place 11 (12, 13) stitches on each of 4 needles.

Join to work in the round, being careful not to twist the stitches.

Place stitch marker for the beginning of the round.

Work 4 rounds in (k1, p1) rib.

ARM

Setup Rounds

Round 1: K0 (1, 2), *p1, k6; work from * twice more for a total of 3 times, p1, knit to end.

Round 2: K0 (1, 2), *p1, 1 over 2 LC, 1 over 2 RC; work from * twice more for a total of 3 times, p1, knit to end.

Working arm as established, knit 0 (1, 2) stitches, work the next 22 stitches in the cable pattern, and knit to the end of the round. Work until rounds 1–5 of cable pattern have been worked a total of 13 times from the beginning, counting the setup rounds in the first repeat.

GUSSET

Left Mitt

Setup round (increase): Work in cable pattern as established to 2 stitches from the end of the round. Place gusset marker, M1L, place gusset marker, k2—1 stitch between gusset markers.

Right Mitt

Setup round (increase): K0 (1, 2), work the next 22 stitches in cable pattern as established, k2 (3, 4), place gusset marker, M1R, place gusset marker, knit to end—1 stitch between gusset markers.

Both Mitts

Rounds 1 and 2: Work as established, knitting the stitches between the gusset markers.

Round 3 (increase): Work as established to first gusset marker, slip marker, M1R, knit to next marker, M1L, slip marker, knit to end—3 stitches between gusset markers.

Work rounds 1-3 above 6 (7, 8) more times, for a total of 7 (8, 9) times—15 (17, 19) stitches between gusset markers.

You will have just completed round 2 (5, 3) of the cable pattern.

TOP OF HAND

Work as established to the first gusset marker, remove marker, place the next 15 (17, 19) stitches on a piece of scrap yarn, remove the second marker, work as established to end.

Working hand as established, knit 0 (1, 2) stitches, work the next 22 stitches in the cable pattern, and knit to the end of the round.

Work rounds 1-5 of cable pattern a total of 19 (20, 21) times from the beginning of the mitt.

Work 4 rounds in (k1, p1) rib.
Bind off loosely in (k1, p1) rib.
Cut the yarn, leaving a tail long enough to weave in.

THUMB

Place the 15 (17, 19) gusset stitches on 3 double-pointed needles, dividing the stitches evenly among the needles.

Round 1: K15 (17, 19), pick up 3 stitches in the gap between the gusset and the hand—18 [20, 22] stitches.

Work 4 rounds in (k1, p1) rib.
Bind off loosely in (k1, p1) rib.
Cut the yarn, leaving a tail long enough to weave in.

FINISHING

Weave in ends.
Block.

CABLE PATTERN

CHART KEY

knit on right side
purl on wrong side

purl on right side
knit on wrong side

slip, with the yarn held in back

1 over 2 RC—Place the next 2 stitches on a cable needle and hold in back. K1, k2 from the cable needle.

1 over 2 LC—Place the next stitch on a cable needle and hold in front. K2, k1 from the cable needle.

repeat

OXBO SOCKS

design by mary lou egan

W arm, thick socks work up quickly. Making these cuff-down socks in two colors is drop-dead easy because keeping track comes naturally. In the simple stitch pattern, the k1, p1 rounds are worked in the main color, while the contrasting-color rounds are always knit. These heavyweight socks keep your fingers warm while knitting and your toes toasty long after.

DIFFICULTY LEVEL
Relaxed

SIZES
Adult S (M, L)

FINISHED MEASUREMENTS
Circumference: 7¾ (8¼, 9)" (19.5 [21, 23]cm) at foot and ankle
Length can be varied to fit the individual foot; see Techniques (page 138) for additional information on sizing socks.

MATERIALS
Two-Color Socks
Berroco Vintage, 50% acrylic, 40% wool, 10% nylon, 3½ oz (100g), 217 yd (198m)
MC: 2 skeins in 51190 Cerulean; CC: 1 skein in 5196 Caramel
One-Color Socks
2 (2, 3) skeins Berroco Vintage, 50% acrylic, 40% wool, 10% nylon, 3½ oz (100g), 217 yd (198m), in 5105 Oats

Both Socks
1 set of 5 US size 5 (3.75mm) double-pointed needles (adjust needle size as necessary to obtain gauge)
Locking stitch markers
Tapestry needle

GAUGE AFTER BLOCKING
25 stitches and 28 rows = 4" (10cm) in stockinette stitch

STITCH PATTERN IN BODY OF PROJECT
Round 1: With CC, knit.
Round 2: With MC, k1, p1.
Repeat these 2 rounds for the pattern.
Note: For One-Color Socks, disregard color specifications throughout pattern.

PATTERN INSTRUCTIONS

CUFF

With MC, cast on 48 (52, 56) stitches. Divide the stitches evenly across 4 needles. Join to work in the round, being careful not to twist the stitches. Place a stitch marker for the beginning of the round. Work (k1, p1) ribbing for 8 rounds.

LEG

Round 1: With CC, knit.
Round 2: With MC, k1, p1.
For One-Color Socks, disregard color specifications throughout the pattern.
Repeat these two rounds for 7" (18cm) or desired length from cast-on edge, ending with round 1 of the pattern. Cut CC yarn, leaving a tail long enough to weave in.

⚠ CONCENTRATION ZONE

HEEL FLAP

Using MC, knit 12 (13, 14) stitches at the beginning of the round, and turn work. Slip first stitch purlwise, purl 23 (25, 27) stitches, turn work. Remove the beginning-of-the-row marker as you come to it. These 24 (26, 28) stitches will be worked back and forth for the heel flap. Arrange the remaining stitches on 2 of the double-pointed needles; these are instep stitches. Arrange the heel flap stitches on 1 needle, setting the remaining needle aside until needed. Continue on this needle for the heel flap as follows:
Row 1 (RS): Slip 1, knit to end of row.
Row 2 (WS): Slip 1, purl to end of row.

Repeat these 2 rows until 24 (26, 28) rows have been completed, including the first row purled before starting the heel flap pattern. End with a right-side row, ready to begin on a wrong-side (purl) row, and turn the heel as follows.
Turn heel:
Row 1 (WS): P14 (15, 16), p2tog, p1, turn.
Row 2 (RS): Slip 1, k5 (5, 5), ssk, k1, turn.
Row 3: Slip 1, p6, p2tog, p1, turn.
Row 4: Slip 1, k7, ssk, k1, turn.
Row 5: Slip 1, p8, p2tog, p1, turn.
Row 6: Slip 1, k9, ssk, k1, turn.
Row 7: Slip 1, p10, p2tog, p1, turn.
Row 8: Slip 1, k11, ssk, k1, turn.
Row 9: Slip 1, p12, p2tog, p0 (1, 1).
Row 10: Slip 1, k12 (13, 13), ssk, k0 (1, 1).
End here for size S—14 stitches remain.

Sizes M and L Only
Row 11: Slip 1, p12, p2tog, p1, turn.
Row 12: Slip 1, k13, ssk, k1. End here for size M—16 stitches remain.

Size L Only
Row 13: Slip 1, p14, p2tog, turn.
Row 14: Slip 1, k14, ssk. End here for size L—16 stitches remain.

HEEL GUSSET
Setup round: With right side facing and continuing with the same double-pointed needle, pick up and knit 12 (13, 14) stitches along the right side of the heel flap. This will become needle 1. With the same needle, pick up and twist the running thread in the gap between the heel flap and the first instep needle, and knit it. This will help prevent a gap at the edge of the instep. Continuing in the round, work the instep stitches in the pattern stitch across what is now needle 2 and needle 3 as established. With needle 4 (the needle that has been set aside), pick up and twist the running thread in the gap between the instep needle and the heel flap and knit it, then pick up and knit 12 (13, 14) stitches along the left side of the heel flap. With the same needle, knit 7 (8, 8) stitches (half of the heel) from the heel flap. Move the remaining 12 (13, 14) stitches by turning the heel onto needle 1 (the needle used to pick up the first side of the gusset). The instep stitches are on needles 2 and 3, and the final needle is needle 4. The first stitch of needle 1 is the beginning of the round. If desired, hang a locking stitch marker on this stitch as a reminder.
Join CC. There should be 24 (26, 28) stitches for the instep and 40 (44, 46) stitches for the sole.

The round now begins in the middle of the heel.

Decrease Gusset
Round 1: With CC, knit.
Round 2: With MC, knit until 3 stitches from instep (end of needle 1), k2tog, k1, work in pattern stitch across instep needles as established (needles 2 and 3), (at start of needle 4) k1, ssk, knit to the end of the round.
Continue working these 2 rounds until there are 48 (52, 56) stitches remaining: 24 (26, 28) stitches for the instep and 24 (26, 28) stitches for the sole.

⌒ CRUISE CONTROL

FOOT
Work as established, with the stitch pattern on the instep and stockinette stitch on the sole of the foot, until foot is about 1½" (3.8cm) less than the desired length. The sample sock shown is 7" (18 cm) long from the heel to the start of the toe. Break off CC yarn. With MC, knit 1 round. The toe is worked in stockinette stitch using MC.

Toe
Round 1: Knit to the last 3 sole stitches before the start of the instep, k2tog, k2, ssk, knit to last 3 instep stitches, k2tog, k2, ssk, knit to the end of the round.
Round 2: Knit.
Work these 2 rounds 5 (6, 6) more times, for a total of 7 (8, 8) times—24 (24, 28) stitches remain. Knit to the beginning of the instep. Cut the yarn, leaving an 18" (45.5cm) tail.
Transfer all of the sole stitches onto one needle and all of the instep stitches onto another needle—12 (12, 14) stitches on each needle. Graft the toe end together using the Kitchener stitch. See Techniques (page 138).

FINISHING
Weave in ends.
Block.

VARIATION: ONE-COLOR SOCK
Work all rounds with MC yarn. You will not have to break the yarn until the end of the sock.

the waiting game

WAITING IS A SYMPTOM OF MODERN LIFE. KNITTING IS our antidote. Portable projects get us through delays, layovers, on-holds, business conferences, and waiting rooms, not to mention the daily commute and car-pool line. These situations require knits that are small enough to tuck away in a pocket and distracting enough to make the time pass—like the Idlewild Socks or the Abide Shawl. The Grand Central Scarf is also perfect for passing time on the go; its secret power is no finishing except for a clever snip of the scissors.

If your work involves participating in long phone conferences or back-to-back meetings, you've got knitting time. If you're like us, keeping your hands going actually helps you focus. These moments call for projects that aren't too flashy, with long stretches of plain old knitting to keep things subtle, like the Keynote Pullover and the Parley Cardigan.

KEYNOTE PULLOVER

design by mary lou egan

Some meetings feel like a death sentence. The doors shut, the PowerPoint begins, and time stands still. Knitting a simple project keeps the part of your brain that would otherwise be planning a barbecue for the weekend occupied. This situation demands an uncomplicated project that is portable and won't draw too much attention. The bottom-up, circular Keynote sweater gives you lots of focus-free knitting while you work the body. The sleeves are worked separately. Later, you can turn your attention to joining the yoke with its stitch pattern.

DIFFICULTY LEVEL
Relaxed

FINISHED MEASUREMENTS
Bust: 32 (34, 36 [38, 40, 42] 44, 46, 48)" (81 [86, 91 (96.5, 101.5, 106.5) 112, 117, 122]cm)
(Shown in size 34)

MATERIALS
5 (5, 6 [7, 7, 7] 8, 8, 9) skeins Berroco Fiora, 40% cotton, 30% rayon, 15% alpaca, 10% nylon 5% wool, 3½ oz (100 g), 246 yd (225m), in 3805 Georgia

1 US size 5 (3.75mm) 32" (80cm) circular needle (adjust needle size as necessary to obtain gauge)
1 US size 5 (3.75mm) 16" (40cm) circular needle *or* 1 set US size 5 (3.75mm) double-pointed needles (adjust needle size as necessary to obtain gauge)
Stitch markers
Scrap yarn
Tapestry needle

GAUGE AFTER BLOCKING
22 stitches and 30 rows = 4" (10cm) in stockinette stitch

STITCH PATTERN
Moiré Stitch (worked in the round over an even number of stitches)
Round 1: *Slip 1, k1, yo, pass slipped stitch over the k1 and the yo; repeat from * to the end of the round.
Rounds 2-4: Knit.
Repeat rounds 1-4 for pattern.

PATTERN NOTES
Sweater is worked from the bottom up in one piece. The sleeves are worked separately and joined to the body before working the yoke.
German short rows are used to shape the back of the neck in this sweater. You may substitute a different short-row method if you wish.

As you work, decrease rounds for the yoke. You may find it necessary to adjust the marker for the beginning of the round by 1 or 2 stitches.

PATTERN INSTRUCTIONS

BODY

On the larger circular needle, cast on 188 (198, 208 [220, 234, 242] 254, 264, 276) stitches. Join to work in the round, being careful not to twist the stitches. Place a stitch marker for the beginning of the round.

Work in stockinette stitch for 18 rounds. Place a marker for shaping: Knit 94 (99, 104 [110, 117, 121] 127, 132, 138), place marker, knit to end of round.

Decrease round: K2tog, knit to 2 stitches after second marker, ssk, slip marker, knit to the end of the round.

Repeat decrease round every 18 rounds 5 (4, 5 [5, 4, 4] 4, 5, 3) more times, for a total of 6 (5, 6 [6, 5, 5] 5, 6, 4) decrease rounds worked—176 (188, 196 [208, 224, 232] 244, 252, 268) stitches.

Work in stockinette stitch until piece measures 16 (17, 17 [17, 18, 18] 18, 18, 18)" (40.5 [43, 43 (43, 45.5, 45.5) 45.5, 45.5, 45.5]cm) from cast-on. On the last round, knit to 4 (4, 4 [5, 5, 5] 6, 6, 6) stitches before the marker at the end of the round. Place these remaining stitches, along with the first 4 (4, 4 [5, 5, 5] 6, 6, 6) unworked stitches of the next round, onto a piece of scrap yarn, removing marker for the beginning of the round as you come to it; 8 (8, 8 [10, 10, 10] 12, 12, 12) stitches total are on the scrap yarn. Do not cut working yarn.

SLEEVE (MAKE 2)

With a separate ball of yarn, using 16" (40cm) circular needle, cast on 46 (48, 48 [48, 48, 50] 50, 54, 54) stitches. Join to work in the round, being careful not to twist the stitches. Place a stitch marker for

the beginning of the round.
Work rounds 1-4 of the moiré pattern 3 times (12 rounds total). Continue in stockinette stitch, as follows:

Increase round: K1, M1L, knit to last stitch before marker, M1R, k1.
Repeat increase round every 12 (12, 12 [11, 11, 10] 9, 10, 8) rounds for a total of 9 (9, 9 [10, 10, 11] 12, 11, 14) increase rounds, counting the initial increase round—64 (66, 66 [68, 68, 72] 74, 78, 82) stitches.

Knit even in stockinette stitch until sleeve measures 16½ (17, 17 [17, 17, 17] 17½, 18, 18)" (42 [43, 43 (43, 43, 43) 44.5, 45.5, 45.5]cm) from cast-on edge, or the desired length to the underarm. On the last round, knit to 4 (4, 4 [5, 5, 5] 6, 6, 6) stitches before the marker at the end of the round.

Place these remaining stitches, along with the first 4 (4, 4 [5, 5, 5] 6, 6, 6) unworked stitches of the next round, onto a piece of scrap yarn for the underarm; 8 (8, 8 [10, 10, 10] 12, 12, 12) stitches total are on the scrap yarn. Cut the working yarn.

Place the remaining 56 (58, 58 [58, 58, 62] 62, 66, 70) stitches on a separate piece of scrap yarn. Set sleeve aside and work the second sleeve. For the second sleeve, after transferring the underarm stitches to scrap yarn and cutting the working yarn, leave the remaining stitches on the needles in preparation to join with the body stitches in the next section.

⚠ CONCENTRATION ZONE

JOIN BODY AND SLEEVES

Beginning at the right sleeve and working with the circular needle that is holding the body stitches and the working yarn previously left

uncut, knit the 56 (58, 58 [58, 58, 62] 62, 66, 70) sleeve stitches from the sleeve needle onto the body needles, place marker for beginning of the round, then knit 40 (43, 45 [47, 51, 53] 55, 57, 61) body stitches, place a marker for center of back, then knit 40 (43, 45 [47, 51, 53] 55, 57, 61) body stitches. Place the next 8 (8, 8 [10, 10, 10] 12, 12, 12) body stitches onto a piece of scrap yarn for the underarm. Place the held sleeve stitches for the remaining sleeve onto a needle and knit them onto the main circular needle, then knit the remaining 80 (86, 90 [94, 102, 106] 110, 114, 122) body stitches. Continue knitting around to the marker at the back of the right sleeve. This is the new beginning of the round—272 (288, 296 [304, 320, 336] 344, 360, 384) stitches.

YOKE

Continuing to work in the round, knit 9 (9, 11 [11, 13, 13] 15, 15, 15) rounds even.
Work rounds 1-4 of moiré pattern 3 times (12 rounds total).
Work 0 (0, 2 [2, 2, 2] 2, 2, 2) rounds even.

First yoke decrease round: *K2, k2tog; repeat from * to end of round—204 (216, 222 [228, 240, 252] 258, 270, 288) stitches.
Work rounds 1-4 of moiré pattern 3 times (12 rounds total).
Work short rows to raise the back of the neck as follows:
Knit 34 (37, 38 [40, 41, 43] 44, 46, 49) stitches past center back, turn, slip 1 stitch, pull yarn firmly over needle to the back to create a double stitch, purl 67 (73, 75 [79, 81, 85] 87, 91, 97) stitches, turn, slip 1, pull yarn firmly over needle to the back to create a double stitch, knit to the beginning of the following round, knitting the two loops of the

double stitch together when you encounter them.

Work 1 (1, 3 [3, 3, 3] 3, 3, 3) rounds even.

Second yoke decrease round:

*K1, k2tog; repeat from * to end of round—136 (144, 148 [152, 160, 168] 172, 180, 192) stitches.

Work rounds 1–4 of moiré pattern 3 times.

Work short rows to raise the back of the neck as follows:

Knit 20 (21, 22 [23, 24, 25] 26, 27, 29) stitches past center back, turn, slip 1 stitch, pull yarn firmly over needle to the back to create a double stitch, purl 39 (41, 43 [45, 47, 49] 51, 53, 57) stitches, turn, slip 1, pull yarn firmly over needle to the back to create a double stitch, knit to the beginning of the following round, knitting the two loops of the double stitch together when you encounter them.

Knit 1 (1, 3 [3, 3, 3] 3, 3, 3) rounds even.

Third yoke decrease round:

For sizes 32 (34, 36, 38)" (81 [86, 91, 96.5]cm) only: *K2, k2tog; repeat from * to end of round—102 (108, 111, 114) stitches.

For sizes 40 (42, 44, 46)" (101.5 [106.5, 112, 117]cm) only: *K1, k2tog; repeat from * to end of round, end k1 (0, 1, 0)—107 (112, 114, 120) stitches.

For size 48" (122cm) only: *K1,

k2tog, k2tog; repeat from * to end
of round, end k2–116 stitches.
For all sizes: Knit rounds 1-4 of
moiré pattern twice.
Knit 7 rounds. Bind off loosely.
Cut the yarn, leaving a tail long
enough to weave in.

FINISHING

Graft underarms as follows:
place the held body stitches on 1
double-pointed needle and the held
underarm stitches onto another
needle. Graft the body stitches to
sleeve stitches using Kitchener
stitch (see Techniques, page 138).
Weave in ends.
Block.

TIP: SLIP AND SLIDE

For holding stitches on the sleeves and underarms, I use narrow ribbon
instead of yarn. Ribbon fits right through the eye of a tapestry needle
and has advantages over yarn for holding stitches: It keeps the stitches
open, making it much easier to slide a needle back into them along with
the ribbon. Once the stitches are on the needle, the ribbon slips out
easily. —MLE

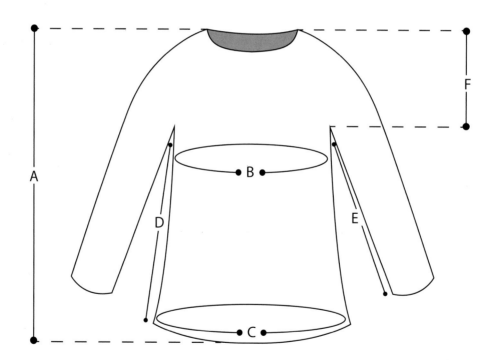

A: 24½ (25½, 26½, 26½, 27¾, 27¾, 28, 28, 28)" (62 [64, 66.5, 66.5, 70, 70, 71, 71, 71]cm)
B: 32 (34, 36, 38, 40, 42, 44, 46, 48)" (81 [86, 91, 96.5, 101.5, 106.5, 112, 117, 122]cm)
C: 34 (36, 38, 40, 42, 44, 46, 48, 50)" (81 [86, 91, 96.5, 101.5, 108, 117, 122, 127]cm)
D: 15 (16, 16, 16, 17, 17, 17, 17, 17)" (38 [40.5, 40.5, 40.5, 43, 43, 43, 43, 43]cm)
E: 16½ (17, 17, 17, 17, 17, 17½, 18, 18)" (42 [43, 43, 43, 43, 43, 44.5, 45.5, 45.5]cm)
F: 9½ (9½, 10½, 10½, 10¾, 10¾, 11, 11, 11)" (24 [24, 26, 26, 27, 27, 28, 28, 28]cm)

PARLEY CARDIGAN

design by mary lou egan

The Parley is the "cardiganized" cousin of the Keynote. The hem uses the yoke stitch for a bit more firmness, and the rest is a breeze. It's also the perfect sweater to wear while waiting—after all, you need an easy-on, easy-off sweater for those overheated and overcooled conference rooms.

DIFFICULTY LEVEL
Attentive

FINISHED MEASUREMENTS
Bust: 32 (34, 36 [38, 40, 42] 44, 46, 48)" (81 [86, 91 (96.5, 101.5, 106.5], 112, 117, 122]cm)
(Shown in size 32)

MATERIALS
3 (3, 4 [4, 4, 5] 5, 5, 5) skeins Briggs & Little Sport, 100% wool, 4 oz (113g), 430 yd (393m), in 75 Mulberry

1 US size 5 (3.75mm) 32" (80cm) circular needle for the body (adjust needle size as necessary to obtain gauge)
1 US size 5 (3.75mm) 16" (40cm) circular needle *or* 1 set double-pointed needles for working sleeves (adjust needle size as necessary to obtain gauge)
1 US size 3 (3.25mm) 24" (60cm) circular needle for button bands (or two sizes smaller than gauge needle)
Stitch markers
Scrap yarn
Tapestry needle
10 buttons, ⅝" (16mm) in diameter

GAUGE AFTER BLOCKING
22 stitches and 30 rows = 4" (10cm) in stockinette stitch

STITCH PATTERNS
Moiré Stitch Worked Flat (worked over an even number of stitches)
  Row 1 (RS): *Slip 1, k1, yo, pass slipped stitch over the k1 and the yo; repeat from * to end of row.
  Row 2 (WS): Purl.
  Row 3 (RS): Knit.
  Row 4 (WS): Purl.
  Repeat rows 1–4 for pattern.

Moiré Stitch Worked in the Round (worked over an even number of stitches)
  Round 1 (RS): *Slip 1, k1, yo, pass slipped stitch over the k1 and the yo; repeat from * to end of round.
  Rounds 2–4 (RS): Knit.
  Repeat rounds 1–4 for pattern.

PATTERN NOTES
The moiré stitch is worked either in the round or flat at various points in the pattern. Take care to follow the appropriate instructions.
Sweater is worked back and forth from the bottom up in one piece on a circular needle. The sleeves are worked separately in the round and joined to the body before working the yoke.
German short rows are used to shape the back of the neck in this sweater. You may substitute a different short-row method if you wish.

PATTERN INSTRUCTIONS

BODY

Cast on 188 (198, 208 [220, 234, 242] 254, 264, 276) stitches.

Purl 1 row.

Work rows 1–4 of the moiré stitch worked flat twice (8 rows total).

Setup row (place markers for shaping and underarm): Knit 47 (49, 52 [55, 58, 60] 63, 66, 69), place marker, knit 94 (100, 104 [110, 118, 122] 128, 132, 138), place marker, knit 47 (49, 52 [55, 58, 60] 63, 66, 69).

Purl 1 row.

Decrease row (RS): Knit to 2 stitches before marker, k2tog, slip marker, knit to second marker, ssk, knit to end of row.

Repeat the decrease row every 9th right-side row 5 (4, 5 [5, 4, 4] 4, 5, 3) more times, for a total of 6 (5, 6 [6, 5, 5] 5, 6, 4) decrease rows worked–176 (188, 196 [208, 224, 232] 244, 252, 268) stitches.

Work in stockinette stitch until the piece measures 16 (17, 17 [17, 18, 18] 18, 18, 18)" (40.5 [43, 43 [43, 45.5, 45.5) 45.5, 45.5, 45.5]cm) from the cast-on edge, ending just having worked a right-side row and ready to begin a wrong-side row.

Next row (WS): Purl to 4 (4, 4 [5, 5, 5] 6, 6, 6) stitches past the first underarm marker.

Place the 8 (8, 8 [10, 10, 10] 12, 12, 12) stitches just worked onto a piece of scrap yarn. Continue to purl to 4 (4, 4 [5, 5, 5] 6, 6, 6) stitches past the second underarm marker. Place the 8 (8, 8 [10, 10, 10] 12, 12, 12) stitches just worked onto a second piece of scrap yarn. Purl to the end of the row. Set aside without cutting the working yarn.

SLEEVE (MAKE 2)

With a separate ball of yarn, and 16" (40cm) circular needle, cast on 46 (48, 48 [48, 48, 50] 50, 54, 54) stitches. Join to work in the round, being careful not to twist the stitches. Place a stitch marker for the beginning of the round.

Work rounds 1–4 of the moiré stitch worked in the round 3 times (12 rounds total).

Increase round: K1, M1L, knit to last stitch before marker, M1R, k1. Continue working in stockinette stitch, repeating the increase round every 12 (12, 12 [11, 11, 10] 9, 10, 8) rounds for a total of 9 (9, 9 [10, 10, 11] 12, 12, 14) increase rounds, including the initial increase round–64 (66, 66 [68, 68, 72] 74, 78, 82) stitches.

Knit even in stockinette stitch until the sleeve measures 16½ (17, 17 [17, 17, 17] 17½, 18, 18)" (42 [43, 43 (43, 43, 43) 44.5, 45.5, 45.5]cm) from the cast-on edge, or the desired length to the underarm. On the last round, knit to 4 (4, 4 [5, 5, 5] 6, 6, 6) stitches before the marker at the end of the round.

Place these remaining stitches, along with the first 4 (4, 4 [5, 5, 5] 6, 6, 6) unworked stitches of the next round, onto a piece of scrap yarn for the underarm: 8 (8, 8 [10, 10, 10] 12, 12, 12) stitches total are on the scrap yarn. Cut working yarn, leaving the tail long enough to weave in.

Place the remaining 56 (58, 58 [58, 58, 62] 62, 66, 70) stitches on a separate piece of scrap yarn. Set this sleeve aside and work the second sleeve. For the second sleeve, after transferring underarm stitches to scrap yarn and cutting the working yarn, leave the remaining stitches on the needle in preparation to join with the body stitches in the next section.

⚠ CONCENTRATION ZONE

JOIN BODY AND SLEEVES

Beginning on the right-hand side of the body, knit to the stitches being held on scrap yarn; leave these for the underarm. Knit the 56 (58, 58 [58, 58, 62] 62, 66, 70) right sleeve stitches onto the circular needle that is holding the body stitches, then knit 43 (46, 48 [50, 54, 56] 58, 60, 63) body stitches, place a marker for the center of the back, and knit the remaining 43 (46, 48 [50, 54, 56] 58, 60, 63) body stitches. Place the held sleeve stitches for the remaining sleeve onto a needle, knit them onto the main circular needle, then knit to the end of the row–272 (288, 296 [304, 320, 336] 344, 360, 384) stitches.

YOKE

Work 7 (7, 9 [9, 11, 11] 13, 13, 13) rows in stockinette stitch, ending with a wrong-side row, ready to start a right-side row.

Work rows 1–4 of moiré stitch worked flat 3 times (12 rows total).

Work 0 (0, 2 [2, 2, 2] 2, 2, 2) rows even.

First yoke decrease row (RS): *K2, k2tog; repeat from * to end of row–204 (216, 222 [228, 240, 252] 258, 270, 288) stitches.

Next row (WS): Purl.

Work rows 1–4 of moiré stitch worked flat 3 times (12 rows total).

Work short rows to raise the back of the neck as follows:

Knit 34 (37, 38 [40, 41, 43] 44, 46, 49) stitches past the center back marker, turn, slip 1 stitch with yarn in front, pull yarn firmly over the needle to the back to create a double stitch, purl 67 (73, 75 [79, 81, 85] 87, 91, 97) stitches, turn, slip 1 stitch with yarn in front, pull yarn firmly over needle to the back to create a double stitch, knit to the end of the row, knitting the two loops of the double stitch together when you encounter them.

Work 1 (1, 3 [3, 3, 3] 3, 3, 3) rows in stockinette, ending having worked a wrong-side row and ready to begin a right-side row, knitting the two loops of the double stitch together when you encounter them.

Second yoke decrease row: *K1, k2tog; repeat from * to end of row—136 (144, 148 [152, 160, 168] 172, 180, 192) stitches.

Work rows 1–4 of moiré stitch worked flat 3 times (12 rows total).

Next row (WS): Purl.

Work short rows to raise the back of the neck as follows:

Knit 20 (21, 22 [23, 24, 25] 26, 27, 29) stitches past center back, turn, slip 1 stitch with yarn in front, pull yarn firmly over needle to the back to create a double stitch, purl 39 (41, 43 [45, 47, 49] 51, 53, 57) stitches, turn, slip 1 stitch with yarn in front, pull yarn firmly over needle to the back to create a double stitch, knit to the end of the row, knitting the two loops of the double stitch together when you encounter them.

Work 1 (1, 3 [3, 3, 3] 3, 3, 3) rows in stockinette, ending having just worked a wrong-side row and ready to begin a right-side row, knitting the two loops of the double stitch together when you encounter them.

Third yoke decrease row:

For sizes 32 (34, 36, 38)" (81 [86, 91, 96.5]cm) only: *K2, k2tog; repeat from * to end of row—102 (108, 111, 114) stitches.

For sizes 40 (42, 44, 46)" (101.5 [106.5, 112, 117]cm) only: *K1, k2tog; repeat from * to end of row—107 (112, 115, 120) stitches.

For size 48" (122cm) only: *K1, k2tog, k2tog; repeat from * to end of row—115 stitches.

Next row for all sizes (WS): Purl.

Knit rows 1–4 of moiré stitch worked flat twice (8 rows total).

Leave stitches on needle.

BUTTON BAND

With smaller circular needle and beginning at bottom right front of cardigan, pick up and knit 138 (146, 146 [146, 146, 156] 156, 156, 156) stitches (approximately 4 stitches for every 5 rows; if you don't pick up this exact number, adjust the buttonhole spacing accordingly). Work in garter stitch (knit every row) for 7 rows.

Bind off.

BUTTONHOLE BAND

With smaller circular needle and beginning at bottom left front of cardigan, pick up and knit 138 (146, 146 [146, 146, 156] 156, 156, 156) stitches. If you adjusted the number of stitches picked up on the button band, pick up and knit the same number for the buttonhole band. Knit 3 rows.

Buttonhole row (RS): K3 (2, 2 [2, 2, 2] 2, 2, 2), *yo, k2tog, k11 (12, 12 [12, 12, 13] 13, 13 13), repeat from * to last 5 (4, 4 [4, 4, 4] 4, 4, 4) stitches, yo, k2tog, knit to end of row.
Knit 3 rows.
Bind off, but do not cut yarn. You should be at the collar end of the button band. With the right side facing, pick up and knit 3 stitches across the top of the button band, knit across the neck stitches previously left live, then pick up and knit 3 stitches across top of right button band. Work in stockinette stitch for 7 rows.

Bind off.
Cut the yarn, leaving a tail long enough to weave in.

FINISHING
Graft underarms as follows:
Place the held body stitches on 1 double-pointed needle and the held underarm stitches onto another needle. Graft the body stitches to sleeve stitches using Kitchener stitch (see Techniques, page 138). Sew buttons onto button band to correspond to buttonholes.
Weave in ends.
Block.

TIP
When picking up stitches around the neckline, use a smaller needle, then switch to the size needle needed for the neckband. To avoid gaps, pick up the number of stitches needed to avoid a hole, then decrease the extra stitches on the first round. —MLE

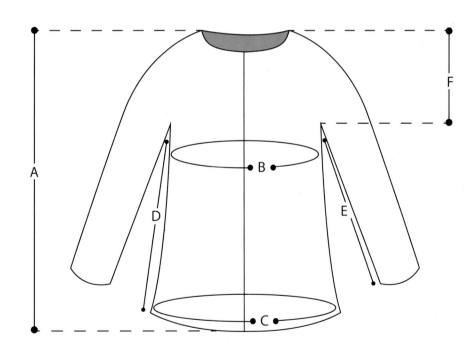

A: 24½ (25½, 26½ [26½, 27¾, 27¾] 28, 28, 28)" (62 [64, 66.5 (66.5, 70, 70) 71, 71, 71]cm)
B: 32 (34, 36 [38, 40, 42] 44, 46, 48)" (81 [86, 91 (96.5, 101.5, 106.5) 112, 117, 122]cm)
C: 34 (36, 38 [40, 42½, 44] 46, 48, 50)" (86 [91, 96.5 (101.5, 108, 117) 122, 127]cm)
D: 15 (16, 16 [16, 17, 17] 17, 17, 17)" (38 [40.5, 40.5 (40.5, 43, 43) 43, 43, 43]cm)
E: 16½ (17, 17 [17, 17, 17] 17½, 18, 18)" (42 [43, 43 (43, 43, 43,) 44.5, 45.5, 45.5]cm)
F: 9½ (9½, 10½ [10½, 10¾, 10¾] 11, 11, 11)" (24 [24, 26 (26, 27, 27) 28, 28, 28]cm)

ABIDE SHAWL

design by kirsten kapur

W e admit it: The first thing we pack when traveling is our knitting. With luggage space at a premium, it's important to choose a project that won't take up a lot of room but will keep us happily knitting throughout our travels. Running out of dresses is OK; running out of knitting is not. The Abide Shawl is the perfect travel game plan. Working in a light fingering-weight yarn, you get a lot of bang for your knitting-time buck. The pretty lace leaf, worked at the same time as the asymmetrical body, looks challenging but is easily memorized within a few repeats.

Attentive

SIZE
One size

FINISHED MEASUREMENTS
Width: 72" (183cm) across top edge
Length: 20" (51cm) from top edge to
point

MATERIALS
1 skein Swans Island Natural Colors
Fingering, 100% organic merino, 3½ oz
(100g), 525 yd (480m), in Vintage
Lilac

1 pair US size 6 (4mm) straight needles
(adjust needle size as necessary to
obtain gauge)
Stitch marker
Tapestry needle

GAUGE AFTER BLOCKING
18 stitches and 32 rows = 4" (10cm) in
garter stitch

SPECIAL STITCHES
Inc 7: Increase 1 stitch to 7.
Knit 1 stitch and leave stitch on left-
hand needle. *Yo, k1 into same stitch;
repeat from * twice more, for a total
of 3 times, and remove stitch from
left-hand needle: 7 stitches have been
created out of 1 stitch.
Make picot: Using a knitted cast-
on (see below), cast on 2 additional

stitches. Bind off 2 stitches, knitting
the stitches in the bind-off through the
back leg.
Knitted cast-on: *Knit the first stitch
on the needle but do not drop the
stitch. Place the stitch just made onto
the left-hand needle. Repeat from *
until the desired number of stitches
have been cast on. To neaten the final
stitch, bring the yarn forward between
the needles before placing the last
stitch on the left-hand needle.

STITCH PATTERNS
Leaf A
Row 1 (RS): Ssk, yo, inc 7, yo, k2tog—
11 stitches in leaf pattern.
Row 2 (WS): Make picot, k1, p7, k2.
Row 3: Ssk, yo, k7, yo, k2tog.
Rows 4 and 5: Repeat rows 2 and 3.
Row 6: Repeat row 2.
Row 7: Ssk, yo, ssk, k3, k2tog, yo,
k2tog—9 stitches in leaf pattern.
Row 8: Make picot, k1, p5, k2.
Row 9: Ssk, yo, ssk, k1, k2tog, yo,
k2tog—7 stitches in leaf pattern.
Row 10: Make picot, k1, p3, k2.
Row 11: Ssk, yo, cdd, yo, k2tog—5
stitches in leaf pattern.
Row 12: Make picot, k1, p1, k2.

Leaf B
Row 1 (RS): Ssk, yo, inc 7, yo, k2tog—
11 stitches in leaf pattern.
Row 2 (WS): Make picot, k1, p7, k1,
k2tog with the next live stitch on the
body of the shawl, turn.

Row 3: Ssk, yo, k7, yo, k2tog.
Rows 4 and 5: Repeat rows 2 and 3.
Row 6: Repeat row 2.
Row 7: Ssk, yo, ssk, k3, k2tog, yo,
k2tog—9 stitches in leaf pattern.
Row 8: Make picot, k1, p5, k1, k2tog
with the next live stitch on the body of
the shawl, turn.
Row 9: Ssk, yo, ssk, k1, k2tog, yo,
k2tog—7 stitches in leaf pattern.
Row 10: Make picot, k1, p3, k1, k2tog
with the next live stitch on the body of
the shawl, turn.
Row 11: Ssk, yo, cdd, yo, k2tog—
5 stitches in leaf pattern.
Row 12: Make picot, k1, p1, k1, k2tog
with the next live stitch on the body of
the shawl, turn.

PATTERN NOTES
Separate stitch counts are occasionally
given for leaf and garter portion of the
shawl body. If not otherwise indicated,
numbers are for total stitch counts.
The body of the shawl is worked in a
4-row repeat. Leaf A is worked along
one edge with a 12-row repeat at the
same time that the body of the shawl is
worked; that is, to work 1 leaf, 3 repeats
of the body pattern must be worked.
Leaf B is worked in a 12-row repeat along
the end of the shawl, attaching it as you
go to the live stitches from the last row
of the shawl body.

PATTERN INSTRUCTIONS

Cast on 4 stitches.

Row 1 (WS): Make picot, knit to end.

Row 2 (increase) (RS): K2, yo, knit to end—5 stitches.

Row 3: Repeat row 1.

Row 4: Knit.

Work rows 1–4 once more—6 stitches.

Work rows 1–3 once more—7 stitches.

ESTABLISH LEAF PATTERN

Row 1 (RS): K2, place marker, work row 1 of Leaf A over the remaining 5 stitches in the row.

Row 2 (WS): Work row 2 of Leaf A over first 11 stitches in the row, slip marker, knit to the end of the row.

Row 3 (increase): K2, yo, slip marker, work row 3 of Leaf A to end—3 stitches to marker, 11 stitches in leaf; 14 stitches total.

Row 4: Work row 4 of Leaf A, slip marker, knit to end.

LEAF A

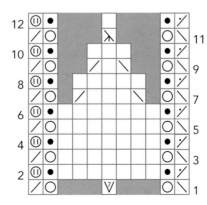

LEAF B

CHART KEY

☐	knit on the right side purl on the wrong side
☐•	purl on the right side knit on the wrong side
O	yo
╱	k2tog
╲	ssk
╱	k2tog with the next live stitch on the body of the shawl
⅄	sk2p
⑪	make picot
ⅴ	inc 7
▨	no stitch

BODY

Row 1 (RS): Knit to marker, slip marker, work Leaf A as established to end.

Row 2 (WS): Work Leaf A as established, slip marker, knit to end.

Row 3 (increase): K2, yo, knit to marker, slip marker, work Leaf A as established to end.

Row 4: Repeat row 2.

Continue to work rows 1-4 above, progressing through all of the rows in Leaf A stitch pattern as you go, until rows 1-12 of Leaf A have been worked a total of 33 times—106 stitches total, 101 stitches to marker, not including Leaf A.

Continuing with the shawl body as established, work rows 1-11 with Leaf A once more, removing the marker on row 11—109 stitches total.

⚠ CONCENTRATION ZONE

Work row 12 of Leaf A, knitting the last stitch of the leaf pattern together with the first stitch on the body of the shawl and stopping at that point. Do not work to the end of the row. Turn work.

FINAL EDGE

Leaf B will be knit onto the live stitches on the end of the shawl by knitting the last stitch of all wrong-side rows of Leaf B together with the next live stitch on the body of the shawl.

Work rows 1-12 of Leaf B a total of 17 times.

⟲ CRUISE CONTROL

Bind off remaining stitches.

FINISHING

Weave in ends.
Block.

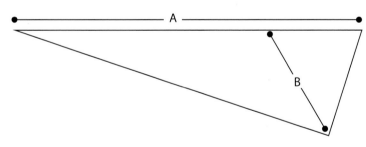

A: 72" (183cm)
B: 20" (51cm)

GRAND CENTRAL SCARF

design by kirsten kapur

Who hasn't finished knitting a project only to set it aside for months, or even years, before weaving in the ends? Guilty! If you're familiar with this never-ending unfinished object scenario, the Grand Central Scarf is the project of your dreams. Knit in the round, this playful scarf makes use of dropped stitches to form the fringe. Drop the stitches, make a quick snip with the scissors, and you're ready to toss it around your neck.

DIFFICULTY LEVEL
Relaxed

SIZES
M (L)

FINISHED MEASUREMENTS
Length: 62½ (75)" (159 [190.5]cm) (excluding fringe)
Width: 6½ (6½)" (16.5 [16.5] cm)

MATERIALS
Zen Yarn Garden Serenity DK, 90% superwash merino, 10% cashmere, 3½ oz (100g), 250 yd (228.5m). MC: 1 skein in Tranquility; CC: 1 skein in Mossy Oak

1 US size 6 (4mm) 40" (100cm) circular needle (adjust needle size as necessary to obtain gauge)
2 stitch markers
Tapestry needle

GAUGE AFTER BLOCKING
20 stitches and 32 rows = 4" (10cm) in stockinette stitch
17 stitches and 36 rows = 4" (10cm) in slipped stitch pattern

STITCH PATTERN
Slipped Stitch Pattern
Multiple of 2 stitches, plus 1.
Rounds 1 and 2: With CC, K1, *slip 1 wyib, k1; repeat from * as directed.
Round 3: With CC, knit.
Round 4: With CC, purl.
Rounds 5-8: Repeat rounds 1-4 using MC.
Repeat rounds 1-8 for pattern.

PATTERN NOTES
This scarf is worked in the round. After knitting the entire scarf, stitches are dropped and cut to create the fringe. Take care not to pull the working yarn tightly behind the slipped stitches as you knit the following stitch to prevent excessive puckering.

PATTERN INSTRUCTIONS

With MC, cast on 301 (355) stitches. Be sure there is at least an 8" (20.5cm) tail after casting on. Join to work in the round, being careful not to twist the stitches. Place a stitch marker for the beginning of the round.
Setup round 1: P271 (325), place marker, k30.
Setup round 2: Knit.
Setup round 3: Purl to marker, slip marker, knit to end.

BODY OF SCARF

Work the first 271 (325) stitches in the slipped stitch pattern, slip marker, knit to the end of the round. Working as established above, work rounds 1–8 of the slipped stitch pattern a total of 6 times.
Cut MC, leaving an 8" (20.5cm) tail. With CC, work rounds 1–4 of the slipped stitch pattern once more. With CC, knit 1 round.
Bind off 271 (325) stitches very loosely using a purled bind-off (see Techniques, page 138). Do not bind off the 30 stitches that have been worked in stockinette stitch.
Cut the yarn, leaving an 8" (20.5cm) tail.

FINISHING

Pull the tail through the stitch on the right-hand needle to secure the end.
Slip the remaining 30 stitches off the needle and unravel them.
Find the center point of the long strands left from the unraveled stitches. Carefully cut the strands at this center point to make fringe of equal lengths on each end of the scarf.

There are groups of fringe of each color. Knot each of these groups at the top, close to the edge of the scarf.
Trim ends of fringe to even them out as necessary.
Block.

IDLEWILD SOCKS

design by kirsten kapur

H aving a pair of in-progress socks tucked in our bag is peace of mind incarnate. It means we're prepared for whatever the day brings, be that a long line at the bank, commute delays, or a committee member who won't cede the floor. For this reason, we offer you the Idlewild Socks. With their easy-to-memorize four-row stitch pattern, they require just enough attention to keep you engaged, but not so much concentration that you miss your stop on the train.

DIFFICULTY LEVEL
Relaxed

SIZES
Adult S (M, L)

FINISHED MEASUREMENTS
Circumference: 6¾ (7½, 8¼)" (17 [19, 21]cm) at foot and ankle
Length can be varied to fit the individual foot; see Techniques (page 138) for additional information on sizing socks.

MATERIALS
1 skein Anzula Squishy 80% superwash merino, 10% cashmere, 10% nylon, 4 oz (114g), 385 yd (352m), in Nimbus

1 set of 5 US size 1 (2.25mm) double-pointed needles (adjust needle size as necessary to obtain gauge)
Stitch markers
Tapestry needle

GAUGE AFTER BLOCKING
32 stitches and 48 rows = 4" (10cm) in stockinette stitch
32 stitches and 48 rows = 4" (10cm) in lace stitch pattern

STITCH PATTERN
Lace Stitch Pattern
Multiple of 6 stitches.
Sizes S and L
Rounds 1 and 2: Knit.
Round 3: *Yo, cdd, yo, k3; repeat from * to end.
Round 4: Purl.
Repeat rounds 1-4 for the pattern.

Size M
Rounds 1 and 2: Knit.
Round 3: K1, *yo, cdd, yo, k3; repeat from * to last 5 stitches, yo, cdd, yo, k2.
Round 4: Purl.
Repeat rounds 1-4 for the pattern.

PATTERN INSTRUCTIONS

CUFF

Cast on 54 (60, 66) stitches. Divide the stitches evenly across 4 needles. Join to work in the round, being careful not to twist the stitches. Place a stitch marker for the beginning of the round.

Rounds 1–12: (K1 tbl, p1) to end.

LEG

Work rounds 1–4 of lace stitch pattern a total of 14 times, or to the desired length from the cast-on edge.

⚠ CONCENTRATION ZONE

HEEL FLAP

Transfer the first 27 (29, 33) stitches onto needle 2, set needle 1 aside to be used again later. Arrange the remaining 27 (31, 33) stitches evenly on needles 3 and 4. Working back and forth across needle 2 only, work the first 27 (29, 33) stitches, following stitch pattern for your chosen size as follows:

Sizes S and L only:

Row 1 (RS): Slip 1 wyif, k1, p1, *k3, p1, k1, p1; repeat from * to end.

Row 2 (WS): Slip 1 wyib, p1, k1, *p3, k1, p1, k1; repeat from* to end.

Size M only:

Row 1 (RS): Slip 1 wyib, *p1, k1, p1, k3; repeat from * to last 4 stitches, (p1, k1) twice.

Row 2 (WS): Slip 1 wyif, *k1, p1, k1, p3; repeat from * to last 4 stitches, (k1, p1) twice.

All sizes:

Continue working these 27 (29, 33) stitches in the heel flap pattern until a total of 30 (32, 34) rows have been completed. End with a wrong-side row, ready to begin on a right-side row and turn the heel.

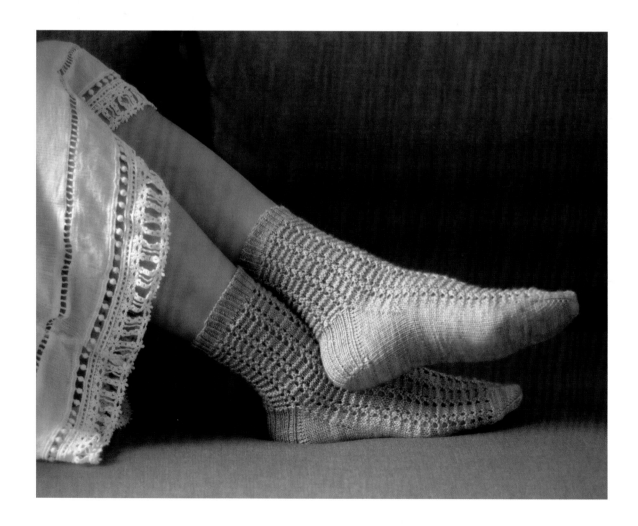

Turn Heel

Row 1: K16 (18, 20), ssk, k1, turn.

Row 2: Slip 1 wyib, p6 (8, 8) p2tog, p1, turn.

Row 3: Slip 1 wyib, k7 (9, 9), ssk, k1, turn.

Row 4: Slip 1 wyib, p8 (10, 10), p2tog, p1, turn.

Row 5: Slip 1 wyib, k9 (11, 11), ssk, k1, turn.

Row 6: Slip 1 wyib, p10 (12, 12), p2tog, p1, turn.

Row 7: Slip 1 wyib, k11 (13, 13), ssk, k1, turn.

Row 8: Slip 1 wyib, p12 (14, 14), p2tog, p1, turn.

Row 9: Slip 1 wyib, k13 (15, 15), ssk, k1, turn.

Row 10: Slip 1 wyib, p14 (16, 16), p2tog, p1, turn. End here for sizes S and M—17 (19) stitches remain on needle 2.

Size L only:

Row 11: Slip 1 wyib, k17, ssk, k1, turn.

Row 12: Slip 1 wyib, p18, p2tog, p1, turn. End here for size L—21 stitches remain on needle 2.

HEEL GUSSET

Setup round: With right side facing, slip 1, k16 (18, 20). Continuing with needle 2, pick up and knit 15 (16, 17) stitches along the right side of the heel flap. With the same needle, pick up and twist the running thread in the gap between the heel flap and the first instep needle, and knit it. This will help prevent a gap at the edge of the instep. Continuing in the round, work the instep stitches in the lace stitch pattern across needles 3 and 4 as established. Place a marker for the end of the instep; this is also the end of the round. With needle 1 (the needle that has been set aside), pick up and twist the running thread in the

gap between the instep needle and the heel flap and knit it, then pick up and knit 15 (16, 17) stitches along the left side of the heel flap. Knit to the instep stitches, then work in pattern as established to end.

There should be 27 (31, 33) stitches for the instep and 49 (53, 57) stitches for the sole. Rearrange the sole stitches evenly across needles 1 and 2.

DECREASE GUSSET

Round 1: Knit across needles 1 and 2, work in lace stitch pattern as established across needles 3 and 4.

Round 2 (decrease): K1, ssk, knit to 3 stitches from the end of needle 2, k2tog, k1, work in lace stitch pattern as established across needles 3 and 4.

Continue working these 2 rounds until there are 54 (60, 66) stitches remaining: 27 (31, 33) stitches for the instep and 27 (29, 33) stitches for the sole.

⟨⟨⟩⟩ CRUISE CONTROL

〰〰〰〰〰〰〰〰〰〰

FOOT

Work as established, working in stockinette stitch across the sole and in the lace stitch pattern across the instep, until foot is about 2 (2¼, 2½)" (5 [5.5, 6.5]cm) less than desired length.

Size M only:

Setup for the toe (decrease): K29 (all of the stitches on needles 1 and 2), k1, ssk, knit to last 3 stitches, k2tog, k1—58 stitches remain: 29 sole stitches and 29 instep stitches. Knit 1 round.

TOE

All sizes:

Round 1 (decrease): K1, ssk, knit to the last 3 sole stitches, k2tog, k2, ssk, knit to the last 3 instep stitches, k2tog, k1.

Round 2: Knit.

Work these 2 rounds 6 (7, 9) more times, for a total of 7 (8, 10) times—26 stitches remain.

Work only round 1 twice—18 stitches remain.

Cut the yarn, leaving an 18" (45.5cm) tail.

Transfer all of the sole stitches onto one needle and all of the instep stitches onto another needle (9 stitches on each needle). Graft the toe end together using the Kitchener stitch (see Techniques, page 138).

FINISHING

Weave in ends.

Block.

drinking buddies

WE CONSIDER OURSELVES THE GO-TO EXPERTS FOR THIS chapter, which could also be called "Knitting with Friends." Whether sharing a house for a weekend getaway or having a knit night with libations, these projects can be knit to gift or to swap. The Shandy Headband and Sharline Boot Toppers are quick to knit in multiples.

This chapter includes designs to create collaboratively with your knitting buddies, like the multicolored Sidekick Hats. Or, in the spirit of a quilting bee, the piecework-inspired squares of Mason-Dixon Knitting's Star-Eyed Julep Throw are knit individually then joined to make a stunning whole. The Galworthy Bag is a gift wrap itself—an item any friend will immediately know was made with love. Lastly, the Lucy and Ethel Cowl is a surefire hit, whether for yourself or a friend who wouldn't hesitate to stomp grapes with you. These projects are all fun knits and easy enough to keep track of while you socialize.

STAR-EYED JULEP THROW

design by kay gardiner and ann shayne
of mason-dixon knitting

This sophisticated but somehow also folksy throw is knit in separate blocks and joined at the end to finish. Whether making the quarters identical, as we show, or following the instructions for a random background, we love this format for knitting a project with our friends. It all comes together with nary a sewing stitch—a three-needle bind-off does the trick—and it makes a wonderful gift for a very special fifth friend, who'll feel the love knit in.

Our Star-Eyed Julep Throw is designed by Kay Gardiner and Ann Shayne of Mason-Dixon Knitting, who can be described as sophisticated but somehow also folksy themselves. Kay and Ann are champions of log cabin knitting, a construction method that's well matched to drop-dead easy qualifiers. It has long stretches of relaxing garter stitch, combined with attention to binding off and picking up stitches to form the squares.

We love that Kay and Ann interpreted a traditional sewn quilt pattern into knitting for us all to enjoy. The throw, like the drink it's named after, is a twist on a traditional classic. Mix a pitcher of this vodka rendition of a mint julep, and hunker down with your friends for some fun throw knitting.

DIFFICULTY LEVEL
Relaxed

SIZE
One size

FINISHED MEASUREMENTS
Approximately 48" x 48" (122cm x 122cm)

MATERIALS
Rowan Pure Wool Superwash Worsted, 100% superwash wool, 1¾ oz (50g), 137 yd (125m)
Center patch color (CPC): 1 skein in 134 Seville
Star point color (SPC): 2 skeins in 133 Gold
Background color 1 (BC1): 4 skeins in 155 Charcoal
Background color 2 (BC2): 4 skeins in 111 Granite
Background color 3 (BC3): 3 skeins in 112 Moonstone

2 US size 6 (4mm) 34" (86cm) circular needles (adjust needle size as necessary to obtain gauge)
1 pair US size 6 (4mm) straight needles for I-cord
Locking stitch marker
Tapestry needle

GAUGE AFTER BLOCKING
18 stitches and 36 rows (18 garter ridges) = 4" (10cm) in garter stitch

PATTERN NOTES
The throw as shown is composed of 4 identical log cabin blocks. For the sample blanket, background colors for the first unit block were selected at random. To create a unique blanket of your own, the same process may be followed. You may randomize the colors in all 4 blocks or just 1, keeping in mind that the quantity of yarn needed will vary from that stated. See directions at the end of the pattern. To create a throw identical to the sample, refer to the schematic.

When picking up stitches along a bound-off edge, pick up 1 stitch for each stitch in the bind-off plus 1 more in the gap at the beginning or end of the row. This is necessary because binding off reduces the number of stitches by 1. Alternatively, increase 1 stitch in the last row before binding off to maintain the proper stitch count.
A garter ridge is formed on the right side by knitting 1 right-side row and 1 wrong-side row.
To work the striped strips, use both background colors indicated on the schematic and alternate one-ridge stripes composed of 2 rows per color to complete the strip.

PATTERN INSTRUCTIONS

BLOCK (MAKE 4)

Center Patch

Using CPC, cast on 9 stitches. Work 18 rows in garter stitch (starting with a right-side row, knit every row) so that you have 9 garter ridges on the right side, ending after having worked a wrong-side row. Mark the right side with a locking stitch marker. Bind off on the right side, leaving the last stitch live. Cut CPC.

Strip 1: Star Point

With the right side facing, orient the piece so that the live stitch remaining after the last bind-off is at the upper right. Using SPC, pick up and knit 9 stitches (1 stitch in the end of each garter ridge).
Next row (WS): Knit to the last 2 stitches (one of which is the stitch that was left live after binding off the center patch), k2tog—9 stitches.
Work these stitches in garter stitch until you have 2 garter ridges on the right side, ending after having worked a wrong-side row. Bind off on the right side, leaving the last stitch live. Do not cut SPC.

Strip 2: Star Point

With the right side facing, orient the piece so that the cast-on edge of the center patch is now at the top and the live stitch remaining after the last bind-off is at the upper right. Using SPC, pick up and knit 11 stitches (1 stitch in the end of each garter ridge of the previous strip and 1 stitch in each loop of the cast-on).
Next row (WS): Knit to the last 2 stitches (one of which is the stitch that was left live after binding off strip 1), k2tog—11 stitches.
Work these stitches in garter stitch until you have 2 garter ridges on the right side, ending after having worked a wrong-side row. Bind off on the right side, leaving the last stitch live. Cut SPC.

Strip 3: Background

With the right side facing, orient the piece so that the live stitch remaining after the last bind-off is at the upper right. Using BC1, pick up and knit 11 stitches (1 stitch in the end of each garter ridge of the previous strip and 1 stitch in the end of each garter ridge of the right edge of the center patch).
Next row (WS): Knit to the last 2 stitches (one of which is the stitch that was left live after binding off strip 2), k2tog—11 stitches.
Work these stitches in garter stitch until you have 7 garter ridges on the right side. Bind off on the right side, leaving the last stitch live. Cut yarn.

Strip 4: Background

With the right side facing, orient the piece so that the bound-off edge of the center patch is now at the top. Using BC1, pick up and knit 18 stitches: 1 stitch in the end of each garter ridge of the previous strip, 1 stitch in each stitch of the bound-off edge of the center patch (see Note, at the beginning of the pattern, on picking up stitches in a bound-off edge), and 1 stitch in the end of each garter ridge of the first strip (the star point to the left of the center patch).

Next row (WS): Knit to the last 2 stitches (one of which is the stitch that was left live after binding off strip 3), k2tog–18 stitches.

Work these stitches in garter stitch until you have 7 garter ridges on the right side, ending after having completed a wrong-side row. Bind off on the right side, leaving the last stitch live. Cut yarn.

COMPLETING THE BLOCK

Using the method of construction described for strips 1–4, continue as established, working 2 garter ridges in SPC on top of each of strips 1 and 2, and working 7 garter ridges in background colors as specified in the schematic on top of each of strips 3 and 4. After completing a total of 10 repeats of strips 1–4 (check stitch counts as you go against the numbers in the schematic), work one more repeat of strips 1 and 2. The last strip should be 101 stitches in length.

JOINING BLOCKS

Using the schematic as a guide, arrange the 4 blocks with the star points all meeting at the center. Join the blocks into horizontal units of 2 blocks each, as follows:

With right side facing and using

SPC, pick up and knit 101 stitches along the edge to be joined. Cut yarn, leaving a tail long enough to weave in.

With right side facing, a new strand of SPC yarn, and the second circular needle, pick up and knit 101 stitches along the joining edge of the second block in the strip. Do not cut yarn.

Arrange the 2 blocks with right sides facing. Slide the stitches to the same end of the needles as the working yarn. Use a three-needle bind-off (see Techniques) to join the 2 blocks. Cut yarn.

Repeat for the second unit of 2 blocks.

JOINING UNITS

Use the schematic as a guide for placement, if desired. With right side facing and using SPC, pick up

and knit 202 stitches in the edges to be joined on each horizontal unit of 2 blocks.

Arrange the stitches of the 2 units, with right side facing, and bind off using the same three-needle bind-off as for joining blocks.

Weave in all ends.

I-CORD EDGING

Using CPC and a straight needle, cast on 3 stitches; use scrap yarn if you plan to graft the I-cord together at the end. Using a second straight needle, insert it into any stitch (or end of garter ridge) on the edge of the blanket to form a stitch on the new needle, then transfer the 3 stitches from the first needle to the left needle. Draw the working yarn across the back of the knitting, and work as follows:

*K2, k2tog through the back of the

loops (thus knitting the last I-cord stitch together with the stitch lifted from the edge of the blanket). With the left needle, pick up a new stitch on the edge of the blanket, return the 3 stitches on the right needle to the left needle; repeat from * until reaching the first corner stitch. Without picking up a stitch from the blanket edge, (slip 3 stitches to left needle, k3) twice. Resume attaching the I-cord to the edge, working 2 rounds unattached at each corner, until you have worked around all 4 edges of the blanket, returning to the starting point.

Note: *You may find it necessary to pick up a stitch in the gap where the blocks have been joined to avoid a hole.*

Bind off the I-cord and cut the yarn, leaving a 12" (30.5cm) tail. Thread the tail on a tapestry needle, and seam the beginning and end of the I-cord together. If you used scrap yarn to cast on the I-cord, do not bind off; instead, undo the cast-on, placing the live stitches back onto the second needle, and use Kitchener stitch to graft the I-cord ends together.

FINISHING
Weave in ends.
Block.

VARIATION:
RANDOM BACKGROUND
BLANKET

For the sample blanket, the color for each background strip was chosen at random for the first block and then repeated for all 4 blocks. If you wish to randomize your entire blanket for more visual interest, write *BC1*, *BC2*, *BC3*, and *Striped Strip* on 4 slips of paper. For each strip, draw 1 slip blindly

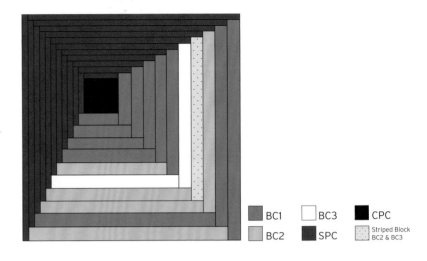

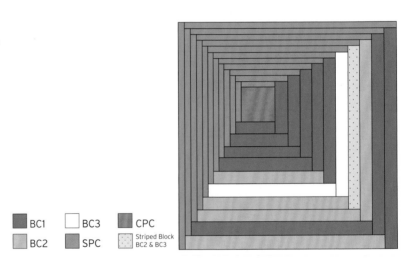

from a bag to designate the color. Use the striped strip just once for each block, randomly choosing which 2 colors to use for this strip. If you run out of any color of yarn, simply remove the slip for that color from the draw. To replicate the sample blanket exactly, refer to the schematic, which notes the color of each strip.

LUCY AND ETHEL COWL

design by kirsten kapur

The body of this cowl features two simple lace patterns. One is worked in two-color stripes; the other, a pretty lace diamond in a single color. Like the duo it's named for, this delightful blend combines to make a fabulous whole. Make this cowl in a yarn that is decadently soft, and you'll find the recipients wearing it all winter long.

DIFFICULTY LEVEL
Relaxed

SIZES
S (L)
Green sample shown (page 58) is size S;
blue sample is size L.

FINISHED MEASUREMENTS
Circumference: 27½ (57)" (70 [145]cm)
Depth: 10" (25.5cm)

MATERIALS
Fibre Company Knightsbridge, 65%
baby llama, 25% merino, 10% silk, 1¾ oz
(50g), 120 yd (110m). MC: 2 (3) skeins
in Cornwall (Concordia); CC: 1 (1) skein in
Barley (Barley)

1 US size 7 (4.5mm) 24 (40)" (60
[100]cm) circular needle (adjust needle
size as necessary to obtain gauge)
Tapestry needle

GAUGE AFTER BLOCKING
14 stitches and 32 rows = 4" (10cm) in
diamond lace pattern
19 stitches and 27 rows = 4" (10cm) in
stockinette stitch

PATTERN NOTES
This cowl is worked in one piece, in the
round.
When alternating yarns in the striped
lace section, it is not necessary to cut
the yarns. Simply carry the yarn up
along the inside of the cowl.

STITCH PATTERNS
Diamond Lace Pattern
Multiple of 8 stitches.
Round 1: *K1, yo, ssk, k5; repeat from *
to end of round.
Round 2 and all even-numbered rounds:
Knit.
Round 3: *K1, yo, k1, ssk, k4; repeat
from * to end of round.

Round 5: *K1, yo, k2, ssk, k3; repeat
from * to end of round.
Round 7: *K1, yo, k3, ssk, k2; repeat
from * to end of round.
Round 9: *K1, yo, k4, ssk, k1; repeat
from * to end of round.
Round 11: *K1, yo, k5, ssk; repeat from *
to end of round.
Round 13: *K6, k2tog, yo; repeat from *
to end of round.
Round 15: *K5, k2tog, k1, yo; repeat
from * to end of round.
Round 17: *K4, k2tog, k2, yo; repeat
from * to end of round.
Round 19: *K3, k2tog, k3, yo; repeat
from * to end of round.
Round 21: *K2, k2tog, k4, yo; repeat
from * to end of round.
Round 23: *K1, k2tog, k5, yo; repeat
from * to end of round.
Round 24: Knit.
Repeat rounds 1-24 for pattern.

PATTERN INSTRUCTIONS

BOTTOM EDGE

With MC, cast on 96 (200) stitches. Join to work in the round, being careful not to twist the stitches. Place a stitch marker for the beginning of the round.

Round 1: Purl.
Round 2: Knit.
Round 3: Purl.

DIAMOND LACE

							24
O						/	23
							22
O					/		21
							20
O				/			19
							18
O			/				17
							16
O		/					15
							14
O	/						13
							12
\						O	11
							10
	\					O	9
							8
		\				O	7
							6
			\			O	5
							4
				\		O	3
							2
					\	O	1

SECTION 1

Work rounds 1-24 of diamond lace pattern, working the stitch pattern 12 (25) times around the circumference of the piece. Work rounds 1-24 once more.

SECTION 2

Join CC.

Striped Lace Pattern

Multiple of 2 stitches

Round 1: With CC, knit.
Round 2: With CC, purl.
Round 3: With MC, knit.
Round 4: With MC, *yo, k2tog; repeat from * to end of round.
Rounds 5-7: Repeat rounds 1-3.
Round 8: With MC, *yo, ssk; repeat from * to end of round.
Repeat rounds 1-8 for pattern.

CHART KEY

☐ knit

Ⓞ yo

◿ k2tog

◺ ssk

☐ repeat

Work rounds 1-8 of striped lace pattern twice.
Work only rounds 1-4 once more. Cut MC, leaving a tail long enough to weave in.

TOP EDGE

Row 1: With CC, purl.
Row 2: With CC, knit.
Row 3: With CC, purl.
Bind off very loosely.

FINISHING

Weave in all ends.
Block.

SIDEKICK HAT

design by mary lou egan

Sharing beverages, sharing a weekend getaway, sharing skeins—we are all about sharing when it comes to our knitting buddies. The simple colorwork in these hats uses small amounts of a delicious yarn. Get together with your friends and purchase multiple skeins, winding off smaller amounts of each color. It's mixology in Rambouillet and alpaca. Woolen spun, not stirred.

DIFFICULTY LEVEL
Relaxed

SIZES
S (M, L)

FINISHED MEASUREMENTS
Head circumference: 18½ (20, 21½)" (47 [51, 55]cm)

MATERIALS
Blue Hat
Swans Island All American Collection Sport, 100% Rambouillet wool, 1½ oz (40g), 185 yd (169m). MC: 1 skein in Ocean; CC: 1 skein in Cloud

Multicolor Hat
Swans Island All American Collection Sport 100% Rambouillet wool, 1½ oz (40g), 185 yd (169m). MC: 1 skein in Ash; CC1: 1 skein in Straw; CC2: 1 skein in Ochre; CC3: 1 skein in Fern

Both Hats
1 US size 2 (2.75mm) 16" (40cm) circular needle for cuff
1 US size 4 (3.5mm) 16" (40cm) circular needle (adjust needle size as necessary to obtain gauge)
1 set US size 4 (3.5mm) double-pointed needles
Stitch markers
Tapestry needle

GAUGE AFTER BLOCKING
26 stitches and 30 rows = 4" (10cm) in stockinette stitch

PATTERN NOTE
If you are new to stranded colorwork, stay loose. Spread the stitches out as you strand to help ensure that the floats are long enough to prevent excess puckering.

PATTERN INSTRUCTIONS

With MC and smaller circular needle cast on 120 (130, 140) stitches. Join to work in the round, being careful not to twist the stitches. Place a stitch marker for the beginning of the round. Work 8 rounds in (k1, p1) rib.

With larger circular needle, work rounds 1-8 of main chart 7 (8, 9) times total. For Multicolor Hat, work first repeat using Ochre as CC (CC2), second repeat using Straw as CC (CC1), and third repeat using Fern as CC (CC3). Continue in this pattern until required number of repeats is completed.

CROWN

Note: As needed, switch to double-pointed needles. For the multicolor hat, begin with the next CC in sequence.

Round 1 (decrease): *K1 in CC, (k2, ssk) in MC, k1 in CC, (k2tog, k2) in MC, repeat from * to the end of the round.

Rounds 2, 4, and 6: Knit even in color pattern as established.

Round 3 (decrease): *K1 in CC, (k2tog, k1) in MC, k1 in CC, (k1, ssk in MC), repeat from * to the end of the round.

Round 5 (decrease): *K1 in MC, k2tog in CC, repeat from *.

Rounds 7 and 8 (decrease): K2tog around in MC.
Cut yarn, leaving an 8" (20.5cm) tail.

MAIN CHART

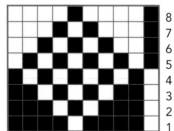

CROWN DECREASES

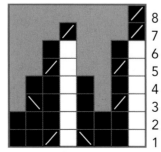

FINISHING

Thread the tail on the tapestry needle, then draw it through the stitches remaining on the needle. Cinch into a tight gather and firmly secure the tail. Weave in ends. Block.
Add pom-pom if desired.

TIP

It is important to work your stranded colorwork gauge swatch in the round, but you can still do it on a smaller number of stitches with a "speed swatch." Use the circular needle but, instead of turning at the end of the row, bring the working yarns to the beginning of the row and knit the next row on the right side each time. Wrap the working yarn around your hand or a couple of fingers to provide some slack to keep the swatch flat. —MLE

CHART KEY

■ knit with MC

□ knit with CC

◩ k2tog with MC

◪ ssk with MC

▨ no stitch

□ repeat

SHARLINE BOOT TOPPERS

design by kirsten kapur

When you're sitting on your favorite barstool, sipping your drink of choice, surrounded by your best knitting friends, you need a project that will get easier as the night wears on. The Sharline Boot Toppers are worked from the top down, so you can get through the lace before you finish your first cocktail. After that, it's easy going with a rib pattern down the leg. You won't want to stop at one pair, so be sure you have enough yarn to make these boot toppers for each of your drinking buddies.

DIFFICULTY LEVEL
Relaxed

SIZES
S (M, L)
Shown in size S worn with 1½" (3.8cm) negative ease

FINISHED MEASUREMENTS
Circumference at cuff: 12½ (14¼, 16)" (32 [36, 40.5]cm)
Circumference at leg (unstretched): 7½ (8½, 9½)" (19 [21.5, 24]cm)
Length: 9" (23cm)

MATERIALS
1 (1, 1) skein Swans Island All American Collection Worsted, 75% Rambouillet wool, 25% alpaca, 2¾ oz (80g), 210 yd (192m), in Kelp

1 set of 5 US size 6 (4mm) double-pointed needles (adjust needle size as necessary to obtain gauge)
Stitch marker
Cable needle
Tapestry needle

GAUGE AFTER BLOCKING
30 stitches and 32 rows = 4" (10cm) in rib pattern, unstretched
18 stitches and 32 rows = 4" (10cm) in stockinette stitch

SPECIAL STITCH
1 over 2 LC: Place the next stitch on a cable needle and hold in front. K2, k1 from the cable needle.

STITCH PATTERN
Rib Pattern
All rounds: *K1, p2, k3, p2; repeat from * to end of round

PATTERN NOTES
These boot toppers are worked in one piece from the top edge down.
The stitch count does not change. Due to the nature of the stitch patterns, the leg becomes narrower in the ribbed area. Select your size based on the cuff measurement with 1-3" (2.5-7.5cm) of negative ease.

PATTERN INSTRUCTIONS

CUFF

Cast on 56 (64, 72) stitches. Place 14 (16, 18) stitches on each of 4 needles. Join to work in the round, being careful not to twist the stitches. Place a stitch marker for the beginning of the round.

Round 1: Purl.
Round 2: Knit.
Round 3: Purl.

⚠ CONCENTRATION ZONE

Work rounds 1–16 of Sharline lace pattern. Work rounds 13–16 once more.

Note: Adjust the stitches as necessary on the needles to complete the decrease and cable stitches.

SHARLINE LACE PATTERN

Multiple of 8 stitches.

Rounds 1, 3, 5, and 7: Knit.
Round 2: *K1, yo, ssk, k3, k2tog, yo; repeat from * to end of round.
Round 4: *K2, yo, ssk, k1, k2tog, yo, k1; repeat from * to end of round.
Round 6: *K3, yo, sk2p, yo, k2; repeat from * to end of round.
Round 8: Repeat round 2.
Round 9: *K1, p1, k5, p1; repeat from * to end of round.
Round 10: *K1, p1, yo, ssk, k1, k2tog, yo, p1; repeat from * to end of round.
Round 11: *K1, p2, k3, p2; repeat from * to end of round.
Round 12: *K1, p2, yo, sk2p, yo, p2; repeat from * to end of round.
Rounds 13–15: Repeat round 11.
Round 16: *K1, p2, 1 over 2 LC, p2; repeat from * to end of round.

⏰ CRUISE CONTROL

LEG

All rounds: *K1, p2, k3, p2; repeat from * to end of round.
Repeat the round above until boot topper measures 9" (23cm) from the cast-on edge.
Bind off very loosely.

FINISHING

Weave in ends from the cuff on the wrong side and ends from the leg on the right side.
Block.

To wear the boot toppers, turn them inside out and fold the cuff to the outside to show off the stitch pattern. Wear them under your favorite boots with the cuff peeking out.

SHARLINE LACE PATTERN

CHART KEY

- ☐ knit on right side
  purl on wrong side
- ● purl on right side
  knit on wrong side
- Ⓞ yo
- ╱ k2tog
- ╲ ssk
- ⋋ sk2p
- ◺◹ 1 over 2 LC–Place the next stitch on a cable needle and hold in front. K2, k1 from the cable needle.
- ☐ repeat

SHANDY HEADBAND

design by kirsten kapur

W hether you are new to lace knitting or an old pro, you'll love making the Shandy Headband. This quick project yields beautiful results with its easy four-row stitch pattern. The headband is worked back and forth and joined with a pair of pretty buttons at the center back. It's perfect for those situations when you want to make multiples of a gift, as an extra group treat at a weekend getaway, or for that moment you find yourself needing to knit something for everyone on the swim team.

DIFFICULTY LEVEL
Relaxed

SIZES
S (M, L)

FINISHED MEASUREMENTS
Circumference: 16 (17, 18)" (40.5 [43, 45.5]cm), buttoned
Width: 2¼" (5.5cm)

MATERIALS
1 skein Lion Brand LB Collection Superwash Merino, 100% superwash merino, 3½ oz (100g), 306 yd (280m), in #170 Dijon

1 pair US size 5 (3.75mm) straight needles (adjust needle size as necessary to obtain gauge)
Tapestry needle
2 buttons, approximately ½" (13mm) in diameter

GAUGE AFTER BLOCKING
13 stitches and 22 rows = 2¼" (5.5cm) in Shandy lace pattern.
24 stitches and 32 rows = 4" (10cm) in stockinette stitch

STITCH PATTERNS
Rib Pattern
  Worked over a multiple of 2 stitches, plus 1.

Row 1 (RS): *K1 tbl, p1; repeat from * to last stitch, k1 tbl.
Row 2 (WS): *P1 tbl, k1; repeat from * to last stitch, p1 tbl.

Shandy Lace Pattern
  Worked over 13 stitches
  Row 1 (RS): K2, yo, k2, ssk, k2tog, k2, yo, k3.
  Rows 2 and 4 (WS): K2, p9, k2.
  Row 3: K3, yo, k2, ssk, k2tog, k2, yo, k2.

PATTERN NOTE
When choosing a size, choose a measurement that is 3-5" (7.5-12.5cm) less than head measurement for a secure fit.

PATTERN INSTRUCTIONS

Cast on 13 stitches.

Work in rib pattern until piece measures 2½" (6.5cm) from cast-on edge. End with a wrong-side row, ready to begin a right-side row.

Work rows 1–4 of Shandy lace pattern until piece measures 14½ (15½, 16½)" (37 [39.5, 42]cm) from cast-on edge. End with a wrong-side row, ready to begin a right-side row.

Work in rib pattern until piece measures 2" (5cm) from beginning of rib. End with a wrong-side row, ready to begin a right-side row.

Buttonhole row (RS): K1 tbl, p1, k1 tbl, yo, k2tog, (p1, k1 tbl) twice, yo, k2tog, p1, k1 tbl.

Next row (WS): *P1 tbl, k1; repeat from * to last stitch, p1 tbl.

Continue in rib as established until piece measures 2½" (6.5cm) from beginning of rib. End with a wrong-side row, ready to begin a right-side row.

Bind off very loosely in (k1, p1) rib.

FINISHING

Weave in all ends.

Block.

Using buttonholes as a guide, sew buttons into place approximately ½" (13mm) from the cast-on end.

TIP

If you've never worked from a chart, this is a great project to try it out. Follow the chart from right to left on the right-side rows, and from left to right on wrong-side rows. Let the row numbers along the sides of the chart be your guide; the numbers are placed on the side where you should begin each row. Be sure to have a close look at the chart key. The symbols for knit and purl will depend on which side of the work you are on. —KAGK

SHANDY LACE CHART

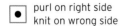

CHART KEY

 knit on right side
purl on wrong side

● purl on right side
knit on wrong side

○ yo

╱ k2tog

╲ ssk

GALWORTHY GIFT BAG

design by kirsten kapur

W hen you want to give a dear friend a gift that shows how much her friendship means, it's all about the details. The Galworthy Gift Bag, with its glimpse of contrasting lining peeking through the eyelets to the beautiful lace top, makes a present memorable, elevating its contents in a way no glittery tissue paper can. Fill it with home-baked cookies, a handknit surprise, or a small bottle of the recipient's favorite liqueur, and your friend will know how much love and care went into her gift.

DIFFICULTY LEVEL
Relaxed

SIZES
S (M, L)
Shown in size M

FINISHED MEASUREMENTS
Circumference: 10½ (13½, 16)" (26.5 [34.5, 40.5]cm)
Height: 6¼" (16cm)

MATERIALS
Neighborhood Fiber Co. Penthouse Silk

Fingering, 100% silk, 4 oz (113g), 500 yd (457m). MC: 1 (1, 1) skein in Woodberry; CC: 1 (1, 1) skein in Del Ray

2 sets of 5 US size 3 (3.25mm) double-pointed needles (adjust needle size as necessary to obtain gauge)
Stitch marker
Tapestry needle

GAUGE AFTER BLOCKING
24 stitches and 36 rows = 4" (10cm) in stockinette stitch

SPECIAL STITCH
Yo twice: Wrap the yarn around the needle twice. When working into these 2 yarn overs on the following row, treat each yarn over as a separate stitch.

PATTERN NOTES
This bag is worked from the bottom up. The exterior shell of the bag and the lining are worked separately and joined before working the top edging. Weave in the ends on the wrong side before joining the 2 pieces.

PATTERN INSTRUCTIONS

BASE OF LINING

⚠ **CONCENTRATION ZONE**

Using CC cast 4 stitches onto one double-pointed needle.

Without turning the work, move the 4 stitches to the opposite end of the needle, ready to work the first stitch that was cast on. Draw the working yarn across the back of all 4 stitches and using a second double-pointed needle, knit the 4 stitches. *Note: The yarn that is drawn across the back of the stitches should be done so snugly. This will prevent a gap between the first and last stitch.*

Again, without turning the work, slip the 4 stitches to the opposite end of the needle, ready to work the first stitch that was knit. Draw the working yarn across the back of all 4 stitches and knit in the front and back of each of the 4 stitches—8 stitches.

Place 2 stitches on each of 4 double-pointed needles.

Place a stitch marker for the beginning of the round. Begin working in the round.

Round 1 (increase): Kfb 8 times—16 stitches (4 stitches on each double-pointed needle).

Round 2: Knit.

Round 3 (increase): Work stitches on the first double-pointed needle as follows: kfb, knit to last stitch on needle, kfb. Repeat for each remaining needle in the round—24 stitches.

Round 4: Knit.

Work rounds 3 and 4 above 5 (7, 9) more times, for a total of 6 (8, 10) times—64 (80, 96) stitches.

⏱ CRUISE CONTROL

BODY OF LINING

Continue working in the round without increasing. Work in stockinette stitch for 40 rounds.

Cut the yarn, leaving a tail long enough to weave in.

Join MC, and work 2 rounds in stockinette.

Cut yarn, leaving a tail long enough to weave in.

Leave the live stitches on the needles.

Weave in all ends. Set aside.

BASE OF EXTERIOR SHELL

⚠ **CONCENTRATION ZONE**

Using MC cast 4 stitches onto one double-pointed needle.

Without turning work, slip the 4 stitches to the opposite end of the needle, ready to work the first stitch that was cast on. Draw the working yarn across the back of all 4 stitches and using a second double-pointed needle, purl the 4 stitches.

Note: The yarn that is drawn across the back of the stitches should be done so snugly. This will prevent a gap between the first and last stitch.

Again, without turning the work, slip the 4 stitches to the opposite end of the needle, ready to work the first stitch that was purled. Draw the working yarn across the back of all 4 stitches and knit in the front and back of each of the 4 stitches—8 stitches.

Place 2 stitches on each of 4 double-pointed needles.

Place a stitch marker for the beginning of the round. Begin working in the round.

Round 1: Purl.

Round 2 (increase): Kfb 8 times—16 stitches (4 stitches on each double-pointed needle).

Round 3: Purl.

Round 4 (increase): Work stitches on the first double-pointed needle as follows: kfb, knit to last stitch on needle, kfb. Repeat for each remaining needle in the round—24 stitches.

Round 5: Purl.

Work rounds 4 and 5 above 5 (7, 9) more times, for a total of 6 (8, 10) times—64 (80, 96) stitches.

⏱ CRUISE CONTROL

Body of Exterior Shell

Continue working in the round, but without increasing.

Rounds 1-7: Knit.

Round 8: *Yo, k2tog; repeat from * to end of round.

Rounds 9-30: Knit.

Round 31: *Ssk, yo twice, k2tog; repeat from * to end of round.

Round 32: *K2, p1, k1; repeat from * to end of round.

Rounds 33-42: Knit.

Do not cut the yarn.

Weave in all ends.

⚠ CONCENTRATION ZONE

JOIN THE LINING TO THE EXTERIOR SHELL

With the stitches still on the needles, turn the lining wrong side out.

Place the lining inside the exterior shell so that the live stitches on each top edge are parallel to one another. The wrong sides of the fabrics should be facing each other. Continuing in the round, knit 1 stitch from the exterior shell together with 1 stitch from the lining. Repeat until all of the exterior shell stitches have been knit together with the lining stitches.

CRUISE CONTROL

TOP OF BAG
Rounds 1–3: Knit.
Round 4 (eyelet round): *K2, yo, k2tog; repeat from * to end of round.
Round 5: Knit.
Round 6: * K1, yo, k2, sk2p, k2, yo; repeat from * to end of round.
Rounds 7, 9, and 11: Knit.
Round 8: *K2, yo, k1, sk2p, k1, yo, k1; repeat from * to end of round.
Round 10: *K3, yo, sk2p, yo, k2; repeat from * to end of round.
Rounds 12–17: Repeat rounds 6–11.
Round 18: Purl.
Round 19: Knit.
Round 20: Purl.
Bind off very loosely.

FINISHING
Weave in all remaining ends.
Block.
Cut six 24" (60cm) lengths of MC.
Knot the pieces together 2" (5cm) from one end.
Group the 6 pieces into 3 pairs of 2 and braid them together until 2" (5cm) remains unbraided. Knot the braid 2" (5cm) from the end to secure it. Trim to even the ends.
Thread the braided cord through the eyelet row.

family entanglements

FAMILY. WHAT'S THAT SAYING? CAN'T LIVE WITH 'EM, can't . . . get together with 'em without knitting! We all know having the right project along can keep you from strangling your relatives—or gives you a thread to connect to others by sharing a little knitting knowledge. The Apple Hill Finger Puppets will charm squirmy youngsters taking their first stab at knitting. The Maplewood Pillow is one of those mesmerizing patterns for knitting while chatting, and it also makes a lovely house gift. If your family is four-footed, the Westerloe Dog Sweater is the most dignified of doggy duds. The Headford Hat is Theresa Gaffey's simple solution to shopping for souvenir yarn when you travel for family gatherings. The Joggle Scarf is like a drinking game for knitters, stitching together your sanity for maximum relaxation at any get-together.

HEADFORD HAT

design by theresa gaffey

W̶e all succumb to the temptation of souvenir skeins. One minute you're a tourist passing by a charming yarn store with no intention of shopping; the next, you're paying for a skein of soft, beautifully dyed wool. To make the best of this habit, when designer Theresa Gaffey travels, she acquires a skein, creates a simple hat, then gives it away en route or stashes it for a hostess present at her destination. The Headford Hat is quality mindless knitting (except for working the top with double-pointed needles). Knit one on your next trip, or knit a batch for gifting. Bonus: When the hats are all similar, there's less squabbling among the cousins and siblings over who got the best one.

DIFFICULTY LEVEL
Mindless

SIZES
S (M, L)

FINISHED MEASUREMENTS
Finished measurement (circumference):
19¼ (20¾, 22½)" (49 [53, 57]cm)

MATERIALS
1 skein Malabrigo Merino Worsted, 100% merino wool, 3½ oz (100g), 210 yd (192m), in 004 Geranio

1 US size 4 (3.5mm) 16" (40cm) circular needle
1 US size 7 (4.5mm) 16" (40cm) circular needle (adjust needle size as necessary to obtain gauge)

1 set of 5 US size 7 (4.5mm) double-pointed needles (adjust needle size as necessary to obtain gauge)
Stitch marker
Tapestry needle

GAUGE AFTER BLOCKING
20 stitches and 30 rows = 4" (10cm) in stockinette stitch

PATTERN INSTRUCTIONS

With smaller circular needle, cast on 88 (96, 104) stitches loosely. Join to work in the round, being careful not to twist the stitches. Place a stitch marker for the beginning of the round.

Work in (k2, p2) ribbing for 2¼" (5.5cm).

Change to the larger circular needle.

Increase round: *K11 (12, 13), M1L, repeat from * to end of round–96, (104, 112) stitches.

Work in stockinette stitch, knitting every round, until hat measures 5 (5¼, 5½)" (12.5 [13.5, 14]cm) from cast-on edge.

CROWN

***Note:** Change to double-pointed needles as necessary.*

Round 1 (decrease): *K10 (11, 12), k2tog, repeat from * to end of round–88 (96, 104) stitches.

Round 2: Knit.

Round 3 (decrease): *K9 (10, 11), k2tog,* repeat from * to end of round.

Round 4: Knit.

Continue working a decrease round followed by an even round, until 32 stitches remain. Each decrease round will have 1 fewer stitch between the decreases than the prior decrease round. When 32 stitches remain, begin working every round as a decrease round until 8 stitches remain.

Cut yarn, leaving an 8" (20.5cm) tail. Thread the tail on the tapestry needle, then draw it through the stitches remaining on the needle. Cinch into a tight gather and firmly secure the tail. Weave in all ends.

JOGGLE SCARF

design by mary lou egan

Attending Thanksgiving, a family reunion, or maybe the mandatory Sunday dinner can feel like death by family gathering. If you need to keep your cool, try this piece of knitting therapy based on the ancient art of the drinking game. The design mixes a solid with a self-striping yarn. The solid is worked in garter stitch, the striping in seed stitch. Choose a cue for changing colors, something specific that pushes your buttons: the cousin who tells the same boring story, the brother who clears his throat in *just that way*. Or maybe it's talk in the royal triumvirate of touchy subjects—politics, sports, and religion. Each time you hear your predetermined cue, change color and texture to create a scarf with a charm that can't be planned.

DIFFICULTY LEVEL
Mindless

SIZE
One size

FINISHED MEASUREMENTS
8½" x 96" (21.5cm x 244cm)

MATERIALS
Classic Elite Liberty Wool, 100% washable wool, 1¾ oz (50g), 122 yd (110m). MC: 2 skeins in #7846 Deep Teal; CC: 3 skeins in #7838 Sunset Frost

1 pair US size 7 (4.5mm) straight needles (adjust needle size as necessary to obtain gauge)
Safety pin or locking stitch marker
Tapestry needle

GAUGE AFTER BLOCKING
20 stitches and 40 rows = 4" (10cm) in garter stitch

PATTERN NOTE
Refer to the pattern introduction for guidance on changing colors to create your own unique scarf.

PATTERN INSTRUCTIONS

With MC, cast on 43 stitches. Knit 1 row. Place a safety pin or stitch marker at the beginning of the next row to indicate the right side. Always change colors on the right side of the scarf.

Knit 6 rows, ending on a wrong-side row, ready to begin a right-side row. Join CC.

Seed Stitch Row: *K1, p1; repeat from * to last stitch, k1.

Work seed stitch row the desired number of times. When ready to work a right-side row, change to MC. Work first MC row in seed stitch. Knit every row with MC the desired number of times.

***Note:** No matter how irritating your nemesis is, work at least 6 rows of one color before changing.*

Continue working as described until scarf is approximately 95½" (242.5cm) long.

End after working a seed stitch section. With MC, knit 6 rows. Bind off.

Weave in ends.

MAPLEWOOD PILLOW

design by kirsten kapur

Tossed on the couch to support Grandpa Frank's head for his afternoon nap or atop the kitchen chair so Cousin Johnny can reach his milk, the Maplewood Pillow is not only pretty, it's useful. Have fun picking colors to make a pillow as unique as your family. Beginning from the center, each side of the Maplewood Pillow is worked in the round out to the edges, where the two pieces are joined together with a three-needle bind-off. After the first few rounds, this pillow will seem easy as pie and be just the thing to work on as you listen to Grandma Ruth tell her old-timey stories.

DIFFICULTY LEVEL
Mindless

SIZE
One size

FINISHED MEASUREMENTS
15" x 15" (38cm x 38cm)
Note: This pillow cover is designed with negative ease so that it will fit snugly on the pillow insert.

MATERIALS
Rowan Pure Wool Worsted, 100% superwash wool, 3½ oz (100g), 219 yd (200m). MC: 1 skein in 131 Mustard; CC1: 2 skeins in 112 Moonstone; CC2: 1 skein in 144 Mallard

2 pairs of US size 7 (4.5mm) 24" (60cm) circular needles (adjust needle size as necessary to obtain gauge)
1 set of 5 US size 7 (4.5mm) double-pointed needles (adjust needle size as necessary to obtain gauge)
4 stitch markers
Tapestry needle
One 18" x 18" (46cm x 46cm) pillow form

GAUGE AFTER BLOCKING
20 stitches and 40 rows = 4" (10cm) in garter stitch

PATTERN NOTES
This pattern is worked in the round, from the center out.
The front and the back are worked separately as Side A and Side B.
The stitches are left live, and the 2 pieces are joined together using a three-needle bind-off.
When colors are alternated every 2 rounds, yarns may be carried up on the wrong side of the work.

PATTERN INSTRUCTIONS

SIDE A

⚠ CONCENTRATION ZONE

Using MC cast 4 stitches onto one double-pointed needle.

Without turning the work, slip the 4 stitches to the opposite end of the needle, ready to work the first stitch that was cast on. Draw the working yarn across the back of all 4 stitches and using a second double-pointed needle, purl the 4 stitches. **Note: The yarn that** **is drawn across the back of the stitches should be done so snugly. This will prevent a gap between the first and last stitch.**

Again, without turning the work, slip the 4 stitches to the opposite end of the needle, ready to work the first stitch that was purled. Draw the working yarn across the back of all 4 stitches and knit in the front and back of each of the 4 stitches—8 stitches.

Place 2 stitches on each of 4 double-pointed needles.

Place a stitch marker for the beginning of the round. Begin working in the round.

Setup for Section 1

Round 1: Purl.

Round 2 (increase): (Kfb) 8 times—16 stitches (4 stitches on each double-pointed needle).

Round 3: Purl.

⏱ CRUISE CONTROL

Section 1

Round 1 (increase): Work stitches on the first double-pointed needle as follows: kfb, knit to last stitch on needle, kfb. Repeat for each remaining needle in the round—24 stitches total.

Round 2: Purl.

Work rounds 1 and 2 above 12 more times, for a total of 13 times—120 stitches.

Note: *Each time round 1 is worked, 8 stitches are added to the total stitch count. When the pillow cover gets too big for the double-pointed needles, switch to a circular needle, placing markers to indicate the location of the increases.*

Upon finishing, cut yarn, leaving a tail long enough to weave in.

Section 2

Join CC1 and work rounds 1 and 2 as established in section 1—128 stitches.

Leave CC1 attached.

Join CC2, and work rounds 1 and 2 as established in section 1—136 stitches.

Leave CC2 attached.

Continue to work as established, alternating colors every 2 rounds.

Work a total of 11 stripes per color, 22 stripes total—296 stitches.

Cut both yarns, leaving tails long enough to weave in.

Set Side A aside, leaving the live stitches on the needles.

SIDE B

Work as described for Side A, except swap the positions of MC and CC2.

When the work becomes too large for the double-pointed needles, switch to the second circular needle.

Once you have completed knitting Side B, leave the live stitches on the needles.

Cut both yarns, leaving tails long enough to weave in.

FINISHING

With wrong sides together and Side B facing you, work a three-needle bind-off (see Techniques, page 138) using CC2 and a spare double-pointed needle for the third needle of the bind-off. Work around 3 sides of the pillow cover, joining them and removing the markers as you encounter them.

Continuing with the three-needle bind-off, bind off the first 35 stitches of the fourth side.

Do not cut the yarn.

Turn the work wrong side out and weave in all ends on the wrong side of the work.

Turn the work back to the right side and steam-block as necessary.

Insert the pillow form into the pillow cover. Continuing with the three-needle bind-off, bind off the remaining stitches.

Cut the yarn, leaving a tail long enough to weave in.

Weave in the remaining end, hiding the end on the wrong side of the pillow cover.

TIP

Want to experiment with color before you begin? This pattern grows from the center out, so you can work the pattern as written until your test swatch is about 4" (10cm) square. Your color experiments will make great coasters, or a fun scarf or blanket when joined.
—KAGK

WESTERLOE DOG SWEATER

design by kirsten kapur

Don't forget to add the family dog to your gift knitting list! She'll be so stylish—not to mention toasty warm—in her Westerloe Dog Sweater. We suggest knitting this project in a washable yarn so there are no worries when the afternoon walk turns into a splash through a puddle or a roll in the mud. The Westerloe Dog Sweater is worked in one piece, from the ribbed turtleneck down to the shaped hem. It features a simple texture of knits and purls across the back to keep your pup looking primo.

DIFFICULTY LEVEL
Relaxed

SIZES
XXS (XS, S, M, L, XL)

FINISHED MEASUREMENTS
Chest circumference: 12 (14, 18, 22, 26, 34)" (30.5 [35.5, 45.5, 56, 66, 86]cm)

MATERIALS
1 (1, 2, 3, 3, 3) skeins Lion Brand Yarns Wool-Ease, 80% acrylic, 20% wool, 3 oz (85g), 197 yd (180m), in 138 Cranberry

All sizes: 1 set of 5 US size 7 (4.5mm) double-pointed needles (adjust needle size as necessary to obtain gauge)

For sizes XXS, XS, S, and M: 1 US size 7 (4.5mm) 16" (40cm) circular needle (adjust needle size as necessary to obtain gauge)

For sizes L and XL: 1 US size 7 (4.5mm) 24" (60cm) circular needle (adjust needle size as necessary to obtain gauge)
Stitch markers
Scrap yarn
Tapestry needle

GAUGE AFTER BLOCKING
20 stitches and 24 rows = 4" (10cm) in waffle pattern
20 stitches and 24 rows = 4" (10cm) in stockinette stitch

STITCH PATTERNS
Waffle Pattern Worked in the Round
 Worked over a multiple of 3 stitches, plus 2.
 Rounds 1 and 2: *P2, k1; repeat from * to last 2 stitches, p2.
 Rounds 3 and 4: Knit.
 Repeat rounds 1-4 for pattern.

Waffle Pattern Worked Flat
 Worked over a multiple of 3 stitches, plus 2.
 Row 1 (RS): *P2, k1; repeat from * to last 2 stitches, p2.
 Row 2 (WS): *K2, p1; repeat from * to last 2 stitches, k2.
 Row 3: Knit.
 Row 4: Purl.
 Repeat rows 1-4 for pattern.

Box continues . . .

PATTERN NOTES
This dog sweater is worked in one piece from the neck down. Double-pointed needles are used for the neck and legs. Switch to the circular needle as needed to accommodate the larger number of stitches in the body and ribbed edging. Select the size based on the chest measurement with 1–3" (2.5–7.5cm) of negative ease.
The length is customizable. Additional yarn may be required if knitted longer than specified.
The waffle pattern is worked either in the round or flat (back and forth) at various points in the pattern. Take care to follow the appropriate instructions.
The waffle pattern is worked between 2 markers to cover the back of the sweater. Regardless of instructions for shaping outside of the 2 markers, work the waffle pattern in order from round/row 1 through round/row 4 consecutively, and maintain pattern as established throughout.

PATTERN INSTRUCTIONS

NECK

Cast on 36 (40, 60, 80, 100, 120) stitches. Place 9 (10, 15, 20, 25, 30) stitches on each of 4 double-pointed needles. Join to work in the round, being careful not to twist the stitches. Place a stitch marker for the beginning of the round, which is also the center of the chest.
Work in (k2, p2) rib for 3 (4, 5, 6, 7, 8)" (7.5 [10, 12.5, 15, 18, 20]cm).

BODY

Setup round 1 (increase): *K6 (4, 6, 8, 10, 6), M1L; repeat from * to end of round—42 (50, 70, 90, 110, 140) stitches.

Setup round 2: K5 (8, 12, 17, 21, 27), place marker, k32 (35, 47, 56, 68, 86), place marker, k5 (7, 11, 17, 21, 27) to end.

Shape Chest

Round 1 (increase): K1, M1L, knit to marker, slip marker, work round 1 of waffle pattern in the round to next marker, slip marker, work to last 1 (0, 0, 0, 1, 1, 1) stitch before end of round, M1R, k1 (0, 0, 1, 1, 1).

Round 2: Knit to marker, slip marker, work round 2 of waffle pattern in the round to next marker, slip marker, knit to end.

Round 3 (increase): K1, M1L, knit to marker, slip marker, work round 3 of waffle pattern in the round to next marker, slip marker, work to last 1 (0, 0, 1, 1, 1) stitch before end of round, M1R, k1 (0, 0, 1, 1, 1).

Round 4: Knit to marker, slip marker, work round 4 of waffle pattern in the round to next marker, slip marker, knit to end.

Work the four rounds above 3 (3, 3, 3, 3, 6) more times, for a total of 4 (4, 4, 4, 4, 7) times—58 (66, 86, 106, 126, 168) stitches.

Sizes XXS and XL only:
Work round 1 only one more time.
Sizes XS, S, M, and L only:
Work rounds 1 to 3 only one more time—60 (70, 90, 110, 130, 170) stitches.

⚠ CONCENTRATION ZONE

CREATE LEG OPENINGS
(All sizes)

Next round: K7 (10, 12, 16, 18, 26), bind off the next 5 (6, 8, 9, 11, 14) stitches, k1, slip marker, work round 2 (4, 4, 4, 4, 2) of waffle pattern in the round to marker, slip marker, k2, place the previous 36 (39, 51, 60, 72, 90) stitches on a piece of scrap yarn, bind off the next 5 (6, 8, 9, 11, 14) stitches, knit to the end of the round. The remaining 14 (19, 23, 32, 36, 52) stitches are the chest stitches.
Work the chest stitches back and forth in stockinette stitch until the piece measures ¾ (1, 1½, 2, 2¼, 2½)" (2 [2.5, 3.8, 5, 5.5, 6.5]cm) from the bind-off for leg openings. End with a wrong-side row, ready to begin a right-side row. Cut the yarn, leaving a tail long enough to weave in. Place these chest stitches on a piece of scrap yarn.
Replace the held stitches on the needles. These are the back stitches. With the right side facing, rejoin the yarn at the right edge of the back stitches.
Working flat (back and forth), work the back stitches as follows. Note: when working rows 1 and 2 below, work rows 1 to 4 of waffle pattern worked flat sequentially beginning with round 3 (1, 1, 1, 1, 3).

Row 1 (RS): K2, slip marker, work in waffle pattern worked flat as established to marker, slip marker, k2.

Row 2 (WS): P2, slip marker, work in waffle pattern worked flat as established to marker, slip marker, p2.

Work rows 1 and 2 above until the piece measures ¾ (1, 1½, 2, 2¼, 2½)" (2 [2.5, 3.8, 5, 5.5, 6.5]cm) from the bind-off for the leg openings. End having just worked a right-side row, ready to cast on stitches across the right leg opening. Make a note of which row of the waffle pattern worked flat you ended on.

LOWER BODY

Round 1: Cast on 5 (6, 8, 9, 11, 14) stitches across the leg opening, place the held chest stitches back on the left needle, and, continuing in the round, knit to the end-of-round marker.

Round 2: Knit to the remaining leg opening, cast on 5 (6, 8, 9, 11, 14) stitches across the leg opening, k2, slip marker, work in waffle pattern in the round to the marker (note: the row numbers of waffle stitch pattern worked flat correspond to the numbers of the waffle stitch pattern worked in the round; for example, if you ended with row 1 of waffle pattern worked flat, you should work round 2 of waffle pattern worked in the round at this point), slip marker, knit to the end of the round–60 (70, 90, 110, 130, 170) stitches.

CRUISE CONTROL

Continue working in the round as established, working the chest stitches in stockinette stitch and the back stitches in waffle pattern in the round, until the piece measures 4 (5, 6, 8, 10½, 11)" (10 [12.5, 15, 20.5, 26.5, 28]cm) from the beginning of the body. Note: You can customize the length of the coat by working more or less at this point. The lower body shaping and rib trim will add 5 (6, 7, 9, 11, 12)" (12.5 [15, 18, 23, 28, 30.5]cm) to the overall length. End with round 1 or 3 of the waffle pattern.

SHAPE LOWER BODY

Note: *Remember that the row numbers of waffle pattern, worked flat, correspond to the round numbers of waffle pattern worked in the round. Once you begin working flat in this section, you should work the row number that is next in the sequence.*

Work as established to 8 (9, 11, 16, 18, 26) stitches before the end of the round.

Bind off the next 16 (19, 23, 32, 36, 52) stitches, removing the beginning marker as you encounter it. Work as established to the end of the row–44 (51, 67, 78, 94, 118) stitches remain.

Turn to continue the back shaping worked flat.

Row 1 (WS): Purl to marker, slip marker, work in waffle pattern worked flat as established, slip marker, purl to the end.

Row 2 (decrease) (RS): K1, ssk, work as established to last 3 stitches, k2tog, k1–42 (49, 65, 76, 92, 116) stitches.

Repeat rows 1 and 2 an additional 3 (5, 7, 8, 10, 13) times, for a total of 4

(6, 8, 9, 11, 14) times–36 (39, 51, 60, 72, 90) stitches.

Work even for 7 rows, working the first and last 2 stitches in stockinette stitch and the stitches between the markers in waffle pattern worked flat as established. On the last row, remove the markers. End with a wrong-side row, ready to begin a right-side row.

FINAL BACK SHAPING

Row 1 (decrease) (RS): K1, ssk, work in waffle pattern worked flat to last 3 stitches, k2tog, k1.

Row 2 (WS): P2, work in waffle pattern worked flat to last 2 stitches, p2–34 (37, 49, 58, 70, 88) stitches.

Repeat rows 1 and 2 an additional 8 (9, 10, 15, 17, 19) times, for a total of

9 (10, 11, 16, 18, 20) times—18 (19, 29, 28, 36, 50) stitches.
Bind off the remaining stitches.

RIB TRIM
With the right side facing and beginning at the right leg, use the circular needle to pick up and knit 16 (19, 23, 32, 36, 52) stitches in the bound-off stitches along the chest, 25 (30, 35, 45, 54, 60) stitches along the left side, 18 (19, 29, 28, 36, 50) stitches along the bound-off stitches on the back, and 25 (30, 35, 45, 54, 60) stitches along the right side—84 (98, 122, 150, 180, 222) stitches.
Work in (k1, p1) rib for 1" (2.5cm). Bind off loosely in rib pattern.

LEGS
With the double-pointed needles, pick up and knit 18 (22, 30, 38, 44, 52) stitches around the leg hole. Divide the stitches evenly on 3 needles.
Work in (k1, p1) rib for 1 (1, 1½, 2, 2¼, 2½)" (2.5 [2.5, 3.8, 5, 5.5, 6.5]cm). Bind off loosely in rib pattern.

FINISHING
Weave in all ends.
Block.

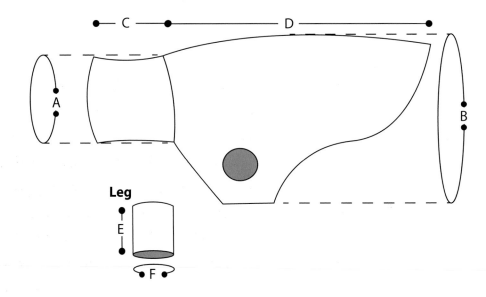

A: 7¼ (8, 12, 16, 20, 24)" (18.5 [20.5, 30.5, 40.5, 51, 61]cm)
B: 12 (14, 18, 22, 26, 34)" (30.5 [35.5, 45.5, 56, 66, 86]cm)
C: 3 (4, 5, 6, 7, 8)" (7.5 [10, 12.5, 15, 18, 21]cm)
D: 10 (12, 14, 18, 21½, 24)" (25.5 [30.5, 35.5, 45.5, 54.5, 61]cm)
E: 1 (1, 1½, 2, 2¼, 2½)" (2.5 [2.5, 3.8, 5, 5.5, 6.5]cm)
F: 3½ (4½, 6¼, 7½, 9, 10½)" (9 [11.5, 16, 19, 23, 26.5]cm)

APPLE HILL FINGER PUPPETS

design by mary lou egan

These beginner-friendly finger puppets were born when Mary Lou was stranded with seven-year-old twins at her sister's house after an ice storm downed the power lines. She had her knitting, of course, so when Nick and Nina wanted to learn to knit, she cast on with some sportweight-yarn bits and helped them work a few rows. The result was the perfect finger puppet. Anything you have on hand will do for embellishment: rickrack, sparkly strings, glittering ribbons. Even black broom straws can make whiskers. The most important thing to remember is to let the child(ren) guide the process and do as much of the work as possible themselves. Don't worry too much about the details—these puppets will be charming no matter what.

DIFFICULTY LEVEL
Mindless

SIZE
To fit most fingers

MATERIALS
For body: 5 yd (4.6m) sportweight wool; the sample used Louet Gems Sport,

100% merino wool, 3½ oz (100g), 225 yd (206m), in #80.2363 Linen Grey
Small amounts of other colors of yarn for embellishment

1 pair US size 4 (3.5mm) straight needles (adjust needle size as necessary to obtain gauge)
Tapestry needle

GAUGE AFTER BLOCKING
20 stitches and 40 rows = 4" (10cm) in garter stitch

PATTERN NOTES
Directions given for making a kitten; use this as a starting point from which your imagination will create many variations.

PATTERN INSTRUCTIONS

Cast on 24 stitches. If desired, leave at least 24" (60cm) of yarn before the cast-on to create a tail later on for your puppet, such as the kitten shown.

Knit 9 rows.

Bind off, leaving another 24" (60cm) of yarn for the kitten's tail, if desired.

Fold in half with the long sides together. Sew the long sides with one of the long tails, first seaming one side, then weaving the yarn across the fold at the top and seaming down the other side. Take the long tails from both the cast-on and the seam and twist the ends to the right. Keep twisting until the yarn bundle begins to kink and fold back on itself, then twist it a little bit more. Make an overhand knot to secure the loose ends, then let the twisted yarns double over on themselves to make a twisted cord, positioning the knot close to the body so you can secure it by stitching it down.

EARS

With a small bit of the body yarn, take a few stitches at each corner and gather them into ears.

Use contrasting colors to embroider the face and whiskers, as desired.

Weave in ends.

Put the puppet on a finger and start the show—then move on to create puppet number two!

bursting with joy

UNLEASH THE ADORABLENESS! WE CAN'T THINK OF A better reason to cast on than a baby in need of a handknit. These projects are easy but sweetly stylish—for infants and little ones. The Polliwog Popover will be in constant use with its happy stripes and smart envelope construction for pulling over the noggin. The simple-to-knit Bambino Blanket and Lambkin Lids are sure to be cherished. Finally, Susan B. Anderson designed the Bear in a Bunny Suit, a softie so cute that everyone in the family will want one.

BAMBINO BLANKET

design by mary lou egan

A baby blanket should be simple to knit, the perfect project to go with binge-watching television or visiting with friends. For this one, we recommend a soft, cozy yarn for snuggling a bambino. Work superwash merino in a simple knit-and-purl square motif, and create a gift that is both classic and modern at the same time.

DIFFICULTY LEVEL
Mindless

SIZE
One size for stroller- or car seat-size blanket

FINISHED MEASUREMENTS
25" x 30" (63.5cm x 76cm)

MATERIALS
5 skeins Plymouth Worsted Merino Superwash, 100% superwash fine merino wool, 3½ oz (100g), 218 yd (199m), in 20 Butter

1 pair US size 7 (4.5mm) straight needles (adjust needle size as necessary to obtain gauge)
2 stitch markers
Tapestry needle

GAUGE AFTER BLOCKING
17 stitches and 28 rows = 4" (10cm) in stockinette stitch

PATTERN INSTRUCTIONS

Cast on 109 stitches.

BOTTOM BORDER
Rows 1-10: Knit.

NEXT ROWS
While working the first row, place a stitch marker after the first 5 stitches and before the last 5 stitches in the row. This will help you to remember to keep these edge stitches in garter stitch. Work the full chart 5 times plus the first 9 stitches of the chart once across the stitches between the markers, as follows:

Rows 1 and 3 (RS): K5, *k9, p9; repeat from * to 9 stitches before marker, k14.

Rows 2 and 4 (WS): K5, *p9, k9; repeat from * to 9 stitches before marker, p9, k5.

Rows 5 and 7: K5, *k3, p3; repeat from * to 3 stitches before marker, k8.

Row 6 and 8: K5, *p3, k3; repeat from * to 3 stitches before marker, end p3, k5.

Rows 9 and 11: Work as for row 1.

Rows 10 and 12: Work as for row 2.

Rows 13 and 15: K5, p9, k9; repeat from * to 9 stitches before marker, p9, k5.

Rows 14 and 16: K5, *k9, p9; repeat from * to 9 stitches before marker, k14.

Rows 17 and 19: K5, *p3, k3; repeat from * to 3 stitches before marker, p3, k5.

Rows 18 and 20: K5, *k3, p3 repeat from * to 3 stitches before marker, k8.

Rows 21 and 23: Work as for row 13.

Rows 22 and 24: Work as for row 14.

Repeat these 24 rows 7 more times, for a total of 8 times. Work rows 1–12 once more.

FINISHING
Bind off.
Weave in ends.
Block.

TOP BORDER
Row 1–10: Knit.

BAMBINO BLANKET CHART

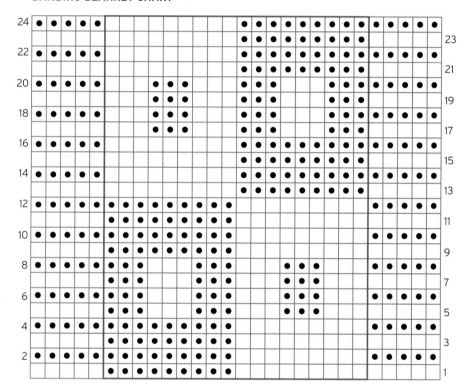

CHART KEY

knit on right side
purl on wrong side

purl on right side
knit on wrong side

repeat

POLLIWOG POPOVER

design by mary lou egan

Babies have giant heads. Anyone who has tried to pull a tight top over a baby knows how challenging it can be. This sweater has overlap shoulders to help your little polliwog get covered up with the least amount of fuss. Soft machine-washable merino wool ensures delicious comfort while knitting *and* wearing.

DIFFICULTY LEVEL
Relaxed

SIZES
6-9 months (9-12 months, 12-24 months)

FINISHED MEASUREMENTS
Chest: 21 (23, 25)" (53.5 [58.5, 63.5]cm)

MATERIALS
Swans Island Washable Wool Merino Sport, 100% organic washable merino wool, 1¾ oz (50g), 180 yd (162m).

MC: 2 (2, 3) skeins in EWB110 Verdigris; CC: 1 (2, 2) skeins in EWB102 Pewter.

1 US size 4 (3.5mm) 24" (60cm) circular needle (adjust needle size as necessary to obtain gauge)
1 set US size 4 (3.5mm) double-pointed needles (adjust needle size as necessary to obtain gauge)
2 stitch markers
Stitch holder or scrap yarn
2 small safety pins or locking stitch markers
Tapestry needle

GAUGE AFTER BLOCKING
24 stitches and 32 rows = 4" (10cm) in stockinette stitch

PATTERN NOTES
German short rows are used to shape the shoulders in this sweater. You may substitute a different short-row method if you wish.
While working stripes, unused yarn may be carried up the inside of the sweater.

PATTERN INSTRUCTIONS

BODY

Cast on 120 (132, 140) stitches. Join to work in the round, being careful not to twist the stitches. Place a stitch marker for the beginning of the round.

With MC, work (k1, p1) ribbing for 8 rounds.

Increase round: K6 (12, 7), M1L, *k12 (12, 14), M1L; repeat from * to last 6 (12, 7) stitches, knit to the end of the round—130 (142, 150) stitches. Knit 2 rounds.

Change to CC, knit 3 rounds.

Continue in stockinette stitch, alternating 3 rounds MC with 3 rounds CC for a total of 17 (18, 20) stripes of each color, ending with a CC stripe.

Cut the CC yarn, leaving a tail long enough to weave in.

Divide for Armholes

With MC, knit 65 (71, 75) stitches. Place remaining 65 (71, 75) stitches on holder or scrap yarn.

You will now be working the front and back, separately, back and forth.

FRONT

Row 1 (WS): P2, *k1, p1; repeat from * to last stitch, p1.

Row 2 (RS): K2, *p1, k1; repeat from * to last stitch, k1.

Work these 2 rows 8 (10, 13) more times, for a total of 18 (22, 28) rows. Work row 1 once more so that you end with a wrong-side row, ready to begin a right-side row.

Begin shoulder shaping, working each side separately.

⚠ CONCENTRATION ZONE

Shape Front Left Shoulder (as worn)

Row 1 (RS): K2, (p1, k1) 13 (14, 16) times total for a short row of 28 (30, 34) stitches. Turn work.

Row 2 (and all WS rows): Slip first stitch, pull yarn firmly over needle to the back to create a double stitch, *k1, p1; repeat from * to last stitch, p1.

Row 3 (RS): K2, (p1, k1) 12 (13, 15) times total for a short row of 26 (28, 32) stitches. Turn work.

Row 5 (RS): K2, (p1, k1) 11 (12, 14) times total for a short row of 24 (26, 30) stitches. Turn work.

Continue working short rows, with each row 2 stitches shorter than the previous row, until 4 stitches remain, ending after a wrong-side row and ready to work a right-side row. Turn, work in pattern to the end of the row, knitting the two loops of the double stitch together when you encounter them. Turn work.

Shape Front Right Shoulder (as worn)

Row 1 (WS): P2, (k1, p1) 13 (14, 16) times total for a short row of 28 (30, 34) stitches. Turn work.

Row 2 (and all RS rows): Slip first stitch, pull yarn firmly over needle to the back to create a double stitch, *p1, k1; repeat from * to last stitch, k1.

Row 3 (WS): P2, (k1, p1) 12 (13, 15) times total for a short row of 26 (28, 32) stitches. Turn work.

Row 5 (WS): P2, (k1, p1) 11 (12, 14) times total for a short row of 24 (26, 30) stitches. Turn work.

Continue working short rows, with each row 2 stitches shorter than the previous row, until 4 stitches remain, ending after a right-side

row and ready to work a wrong-side row. Turn, work in pattern to the end of the row, knitting the two loops of the double stitch together when you encounter them.

Work a sewn bind-off over the (k1, p1) ribbing as described in the Techniques section.

Note: Work the first 2 knit stitches and the last 2 knit stitches as though they were 1 stitch for the purposes of the bind-off.

Place a safety pin or locking stitch marker 16 (18, 20) rows above the beginning of the ribbing on both the right and left edges of the front of the sweater. This will mark the spot for the shoulder overlap.

BACK

Transfer the held stitches to needles. Join MC, ready to work a wrong-side row.

Row 1 (WS): P2, *k1, p1; repeat from * to last stitch, p1.

Row 2 (RS): K2, *p1, k1; repeat from * to last stitch, k1.

Work these 2 rows 12 (14, 17) more times, for a total of 26 (30, 36) rows. Work row 1 once more so that you end with a wrong-side row, ready to begin on a right-side row. Begin shoulder shaping, working each side separately.

Shape Back Right Shoulder (as worn)

Row 1 (RS): K2, (p1, k1) 12 (13, 15) times total for a short row of 26 (28, 32) stitches. Turn work.

Row 2 (and all WS rows): Slip first stitch, pull yarn firmly over needle to the back to create a double stitch, *p1, k1; repeat from * to last stitch, p1.

Row 3 (RS): K2, (p1, k1) 11 (12, 14) times total for a short row of 24 (26, 30) stitches. Turn work.

Row 5 (RS): K2, (p1, k1) 10 (11, 13) times total for a short row of 22 (24, 28) stitches. Turn work.

Continue working short rows, with each row 2 stitches shorter than the previous row, until 4 stitches remain, ending after a wrong-side row and ready to work a right-side row. Turn, work in pattern to the end of the row, knitting the two loops of the double stitch together when you encounter them.

Shape Back Left Shoulder (as worn)

Row 1 (WS): P2, (k1, p1) 12 (13, 15) times total for a short row of 26 (28, 32) stitches. Turn work.

Row 2 (and all RS rows): Slip first stitch, pull yarn firmly over needle to the back to create a double stitch, *p1, k1; repeat from * to last stitch, k1.

Row 3 (WS): P2, (k1, p1) 11 (12, 14) times total for a short row of 24 (26, 30) stitches. Turn work.

Row 5 (WS): P2, (k1, p1) 10 (11, 13) times total for a short row of 22 (24, 28) stitches. Turn work.

Continue working short rows, with each row 2 stitches shorter than the previous row, until 4 stitches remain, ending after a right-side row and ready to work a wrong-side row. Turn, work in pattern to the end of the row, knitting the two loops of the double stitch together when you encounter them. Work a sewn bind-off over the

(k1, p1) ribbing as described in the Techniques section (page 138).
Note: Work the first 2 knit stitches and the last 2 knit stitches as though they were 1 stitch for the purposes of the bind-off.

SLEEVE

Overlap the back shoulders over the front shoulders. Pin the tip of the back shoulders down at the markers placed along the left and right front edges to mark the overlap. Pin both sides in place.

With CC and double-pointed needles, starting at the division between the front and back of the sweater, pick up 54 (58, 60) stitches around the armhole, going through both thicknesses at the shoulders. Place a marker for the beginning of the round. Knit 3 rounds even.

CRUISE CONTROL

Join MC. Knit 3 rounds even. Continue in stripe pattern of 3 rows CC alternated with 3 rows MC while, at the same time, working decreases as follows:

Rounds 1–5: Work even (CC for first 3 rounds, MC for last 2).
Round 6: (MC) K1, k2tog, work to last 3 stitches, k2tog tbl, k1.
Repeat rounds 1–6 another 6 (7, 7) times, for a total of 7 (8, 8) times and 14 (16, 16) stitches

decreased—40 (42, 44) stitches. Work even in stripe pattern as established for an additional 3 (3, 9) rounds.
Cut the CC yarn, leaving a tail long enough to weave in.
With MC, k4 (6, 5), *k2tog, k8 (8, 9); repeat from * to last 6 stitches, k2tog, k4–36 (38, 40) stitches.
Work in (k1, p1) rib for 6 rounds.
Work a sewn bind-off over the (k1, p1) ribbing as described in the Techniques section (page 138).

FINISHING
Weave in ends.
Block.

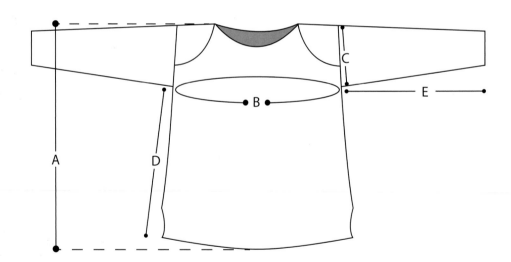

A: 10 (10½, 11¼)" (25.5 [26.6, 28.3]cm)
B: 21 (23, 25)" (53.5 [58.5, 63.5]cm)
C: 4½ (4¾, 5)" (11.5 [12, 12.5]cm)
D: 5½ (5¾, 6¼)" (14 [14.6, 15.8]cm)
E: 6½ (7¼, 8)" (16.5 [18.5, 8]cm)

BEAR IN A BUNNY SUIT

design by susan b. anderson

When we asked Susan B. Anderson to design a toy for us, we knew it'd be sweet and cute—but not cutesy. Sure enough, she created the Bear in a Bunny Suit and we're officially smitten. This little bear has all the details that make Susan's toy designs special, including a bunny-eared hood that comes off the head but stays attached at the neck. If you're new to knitting with double-pointed needles, this is a fun little project to help develop your skills. The miracle of stuffing and fluffing a finished toy hides any small imperfections. It's guaranteed to be lovable when finished.

DIFFICULTY LEVEL
Relaxed

SIZE
One size

FINISHED MEASUREMENTS
Approximately 5½" (14cm) tall

MATERIALS
Quince & Co. Owl, 50% American wool, 50% New Zealand alpaca, 1¾ oz (50g), 120 yd (110m). Bunny Suit: 1 skein in Cielo; Bear: 1 skein in Tawny

1 set of 4 US size 5 (3.75mm) double-pointed needles (adjust needle size as necessary to obtain gauge)

2 locking stitch markers
Tapestry needle
Scrap yarn
Polyester fiberfill
Two ¼" (6mm) safety eyes or buttons
Small amount of brown worsted-weight yarn for the face embroidery

GAUGE AFTER BLOCKING
22 stitches and 28 rows = 4" (10cm) in stockinette stitch

PATTERN NOTES
Buttons are considered a choking hazard for babies and children under the age of 5 years old. Embroider or use safety eyes if there is any concern.
Gauge is not critical to this pattern, though it should be tight enough to prevent the stuffing from showing through the fabric. If gauge varies from that specified, the size of the toy and the yarn yardage required will also vary. The hood is knitted back and forth directly from the body of the toy on stitches that are created and held on scrap yarn while the body is knit. Bear ear placement is indicated with purl stitches on the head. Place the bunny-hood ears and the bear arms and legs following instructions in pattern and as indicated in photos.

PATTERN INSTRUCTIONS

BODY

Starting at the bottom of the body and in the Bunny Suit color, cast on 9 stitches, leaving a tail that is at least 8" (20.5cm) long. Place 3 stitches on each of 3 double-pointed needles. Join to work in the round, being careful not to twist the stitches. Place a stitch marker on the first stitch to mark the beginning of the round.

Round 1: Knit.

Round 2: Kfb in each stitch—6 stitches per needle, 18 stitches total.

Round 3: Knit.

Round 4: *K1, kfb; repeat from * to the end of the round—9 stitches per needle, 27 stitches total.

Round 5: Knit.

Round 6: *K2, kfb; repeat from * to the end of the round—12 stitches per needle, 36 stitches total.

Round 7: Knit.

Round 8: *K3, kfb; repeat from * to the end of the round—15 stitches per needle, 45 stitches total.

Rounds 9 and 10: Knit.

Move the stitch marker to the first stitch on round 10 and leave it there to guide the head and hood placement. Continue to knit every round until the body measures 2½" (6.5cm) above the stitch marker on round 10.

At this point, thread the tapestry needle with the tail from the cast-on stitches. Insert the tapestry needle through each of the cast-on stitches, and pull the yarn through to snugly gather and close the hole at the bottom of the body. Pull the end to the wrong side, weave in, and trim.

Round 1 (decrease): *K3, k2tog; repeat from * to the end of the round—12 stitches per needle, 36 stitches total.

Round 2: Knit.

Round 3 (decrease): *K2, k2tog; repeat from * to the end of the round—9 stitches per needle, 27 stitches total.

Rounds 4 and 5: Knit.

Begin stuffing the body with fiberfill. Stuff until the body is firm but remains squishy. Do not overstuff. Continue to add stuffing as you work until the body is closed.

Round 6: Kfb in each stitch around—18 stitches per needle, 54 stitches total.

Round 7: Thread a tapestry needle with scrap yarn. *K1, place the next stitch on the scrap yarn (holding scrap yarn to the front of the work); repeat from * to the end of the round. The held stitches will be picked back up later for the hood—9 stitches per needle, 27 stitches total on needles, 27 stitches held on scrap yarn.

Change to the Bear yarn color.

Round 8: *K1, k2tog; repeat from * to the end of the round—6 stitches per needle, 18 stitches total.

Rounds 9 and 10: Knit.

Round 11: K2tog to the end of the round—3 stitches per needle, 9 stitches total.

Finish stuffing, if needed.

Cut the yarn, leaving an 8" (20.5cm) tail. Thread the tail on the tapestry needle, and then draw the yarn through the stitches left on needles. Cinch into a tight gather. Run the tail through the loops once more to secure it. Do not cut the tail, leave it out to be used later. Leave the stitch marker attached to the first stitch of the round to mark the front of the body.

HEAD

Starting at the back of the head and in the Bear color, cast on 9 stitches, placing 3 stitches on each of 3 double-pointed needles. Join to work in the round, being careful not to twist the stitches. Place a stitch marker on the first stitch to mark the beginning of the round.

Round 1: Knit.

Round 2: Kfb in each stitch around—6 stitches per needle, 18 stitches total.

Round 3: Knit.

Round 4: *K1, kfb; repeat from * to the end of the round—9 stitches per needle, 27 stitches total.

Round 5: Knit.

Round 6: *K2, kfb; repeat from * to the end of the round—12 stitches per needle, 36 stitches total.

Round 7: Knit.

Round 8: *K5, kfb; repeat from * to the end of the round—14 stitches per needle, 42 stitches total

Round 9: Knit.

Move the stitch marker to the first stitch of round 9 and leave it there. Continue to knit every round until the head measures ¾" (2cm) above the round 9 stitch marker.

Round 10: Work purl stitches to mark ear placement as follows:

Needle 1: K3, p6, k5.

Needle 2: Knit.

Needle 3: K5, p6, k3.

Continue to knit every round until the head measures 1½" (3.8cm) above the round 9 stitch marker.

SHAPE FACE

Round 1 (decrease): *K5, k2tog; repeat from * to the end of the round—12 stitches per needle, 36 stitches total.

Round 2: Knit.

Round 3 (decrease): *K4, k2tog; repeat from * to the end of the round—10 stitches per needle, 30 stitches total.

Rounds 4 and 5: Knit.

At this point, thread the tapestry needle with the tail from the cast-

Round 12: Knit.
Finish adding any stuffing; the head should be firm but squishy. Cut the yarn, leaving an 8" (20.5cm) tail. Thread the tail on the tapestry needle and draw the yarn through stitches left on the knitting needle. Cinch into a tight gather. Pull the end to the wrong side, weave in, and trim.

Face and Eyes

Thread the tapestry needle with brown worsted-weight yarn. Work 5 horizontal stitches over the gathered hole for the nose, going in and out of the same stitch on each side, as pictured. Following the photos for guidance, make a straight stitch going down from the center of the nose and a V at the base of the straight stitch for the smile.
If using buttons for eyes, sew them firmly in place. (See Pattern Notes, above, on choking hazards for young children.)

ATTACH HEAD

Thread the tail left out at the top of the body onto a tapestry needle. Firmly whipstitch the head to the body inside the stitches held for the hood, being careful not to sew over the held stitches. Place the head so that the face is centered above the stitch marker left on the body that indicates the beginning of the round. If the head is too wobbly after one time around, stitch around a second time in a larger circle. Pull the end to the wrong side, weave in, and trim.

EARS

With the back of the head facing you, insert the tip of one double-pointed needle under the right leg of the 6 consecutive stitches

on stitches. Thread the tapestry needle through the cast-on stitches and pull the tail snugly to gather and close the hole at the back of the head. Pull the tail to the wrong side, weave in the end, and trim. Begin stuffing the head with fiberfill; it should be firm but remain a bit squishy. Do not overstuff.
Round 6 (decrease): *K3, k2tog; repeat from * to the end of the round—8 stitches per needle, 24 stitches total.
Rounds 7 and 8: Knit.
Round 9 (decrease): *K2, k2tog;

repeat from * to the end of the round—6 stitches per needle, 18 stitches total.
Note: Continue to add stuffing as you work until the head is closed.
Round 10: Knit.
Note: If you are using safety eyes, set them in place and attach them at this point, following the manufacturer's instructions. Place them 5 stitches apart, just after round 6.
Round 11 (decrease): K2tog to the end of the round—3 stitches per needle, 9 stitches total.

directly below the 6 purled ear-placement stitches. Skip the purl row. With a second double-pointed needle, insert the needle under the right leg of 6 consecutive stitches directly above the purled ear-placement stitches. You will be knitting in the round on 2 double-pointed needles—6 stitches on each of 2 double-pointed needles, 12 stitches total.

With the back of the head facing you, continue working with the Bear color, leaving a 4" (10cm) tail to weave in later. Place a stitch marker on the first stitch.

Rounds 1 and 2: Knit.

Round 3: *K1, ssk, k2tog, k1; repeat from * on each needle—4 stitches per needle, 8 stitches total.

Round 4: *K1, k2tog, k1; repeat from * on each needle—3 stitches per needle, 6 stitches total.

Cut the yarn, leaving an 8" (20.5cm) tail. Thread the tail on the tapestry needle and then draw the yarn through the stitches remaining on the knitting needle. Cinch into a tight gather. Pull the end to the wrong side, weave in, and trim. Repeat to make second ear.

HOOD

Place the 27 stitches being held on scrap yarn onto 3 double-pointed needles (9 stitches per needle), starting at the center front of the body, as indicated by the stitch marker. Reattach the Bunny Suit color and work back and forth on the 3 double-pointed needles. Work in stockinette stitch, starting on the needle where the marker indicates the front of the body. This is the first needle, and you will start with a knit row.

Row 1 (RS): *K2, kfb; repeat from * to the end of the row—12 stitches per needle, 36 stitches total.

Row 2 (WS): K3, purl to the last 3 stitches at the end of the row, k3.

Row 3: *K5, kfb; repeat from * to the end of the row—14 stitches per needle, 42 stitches total.

Row 4: K3, purl to the last 3 stitches at the end of the row, k3.

Row 5: Knit.

Repeat rows 4 and 5 until the hood measures 3½" (9cm) above the picked-up stitches. End after having worked row 4.

Shape Top of Hood

Row 1: K14, then k2tog 7 times, k14—35 stitches.

Row 2: K3, p14, p2tog, p13, k3—34 stitches.

Place 17 stitches on each of 2 double-pointed needles. Cut the yarn, leaving a 16" (40.5cm) tail. Graft the top of the hood together using the Kitchener stitch (see Techniques, page 138). Weave the end in on the wrong side and trim.

Bunny Ears

Place the hood on the Bear's head. Leaving an 8" (20.5cm) end and starting 1" (2.5cm) back from the front edge of the hood and on the 3rd row down from the top seam, pick up 6 stitches by inserting the tip of a double-pointed needle under the right leg of 6 consecutive stitches. Skip a row and, directly under the 6 stitches on the first double-pointed needle, pick up 6 consecutive stitches in the same way with a second double-pointed needle—6 stitches on each of 2 double-pointed needles, 12 stitches total.

Using the Bunny Suit color, begin working in the round on 2 double-pointed needles as follows:

Rounds 1-3: Knit.

Round 4: *K3, kfb; repeat from * to the end of the round—15 stitches.

Work the next round onto 3 double-pointed needles with 5 stitches on each needle.

Knit every round until the ear measures 3" (7.5cm) from the picked-up stitches.

Shape Top of Ear

Round 1 (decrease): *K3, k2tog; repeat from * to the end of the round—12 stitches.

Round 2: Knit.

Round 3 (decrease): *K2, k2tog; repeat from * to the end of the round—9 stitches.

Cut the yarn, leaving an 8" (20.5cm) tail. Thread the tail on the tapestry needle and then draw the yarn through the stitches remaining on the knitting needle. Cinch into a tight gather. Pull the tail to the wrong side and trim. Thread a tapestry needle with the tail at the base of the ear. Pinch the base of the ear so the sides touch. Using the tapestry needle, make 3 stitches to hold the sides of the ear together at the base of the ear. Pull the end to the wrong side and trim so the end stays hidden on the wrong side. Repeat on the other side of the hood seam for the second ear. Steam the hood so the edging lies flat and to relax the ears, if needed.

ARMS

Starting directly under the hood and 1 stitch back from the hood border, pick up 6 stitches by inserting the tip of a double-pointed needle under the right leg of 6 consecutive stitches. Skip a row and, directly under the 6 stitches on the first double-pointed needle, pick up 6 consecutive stitches in the same way with a second double-pointed needle—12 stitches. Begin working in the round on 2 double-pointed needles with the

Bunny Suit color. Start on the bottom double-pointed needle and mark the first stitch with a locking stitch marker.

Rounds 1 and 2: Knit.

Round 3: *K3, kfb; repeat from * to the end of the round—15 stitches. Evenly divide the stitches onto 3 double-pointed needles—5 stitches per needle.

Knit every round for 1½" (3.8cm) above the picked-up stitches.

Decrease round: *K3, k2tog; repeat from * to the end of the round—4 stitches per needle, 12 stitches total.

Next round: *K1, p1; repeat from * to the end of the round.

Stuff the arm lightly with fiberfill. Switch to the Bear color.

Hands

Round 1: Knit.

Round 2: *K1, kfb; repeat from * to the end of the round—6 stitches per needle, 18 stitches total.

Rounds 3–5: Knit.

Round 6: *K1, k2tog; repeat from * to the end of the round—4 stitches per needle, 12 stitches total.

Round 7: Knit.

Stuff the hand lightly with fiberfill.

Round 8: *K1, k2tog, k1; repeat from * on each needle—3 stitches per needle, 9 stitches total.

Cut the yarn, leaving an 8" (20.5cm) tail. Thread the tail on the tapestry needle and draw the yarn through the stitches remaining on the knitting needle. Cinch into a tight gather. Pull the tail to the wrong side and trim.

Repeat for the second arm on the other side.

LEGS

With a locking stitch marker, mark the center stitch in the round just after the increase rounds on the bottom and front of the body. Starting in the second stitch to the right of the marked center stitch and working away from it, pick up 7 stitches on one double-pointed needle by inserting the tip under the right leg of 7 consecutive stitches. Skip a row of stitches and pick up 7 stitches in the same way directly below the 7 stitches on the top double-pointed needle—14 stitches.

Using the Bunny Suit color, work in the round on 2 double-pointed needles. Start on the bottom needle and mark the first stitch with a locking stitch marker.

Rounds 1 and 2: Knit.

Work an increase round as follows:

Needle 1: Kfb, k2, kfb, k2, kfb—10 stitches.

Needle 2: K3, kfb, k3—8 stitches.

Evenly distribute the stitches onto 3 double-pointed needles (6 stitches per needle).

Knit every round until the leg measures 1" (2.5cm) from the picked-up stitches.

Decrease round: *K1, k2tog; repeat from * to the end of the round—4 stitches per needle, 12 stitches total.

Next round: *K1, p1; repeat from * to the end of the round.

Stuff the leg lightly with fiberfill. Switch to the Bear color.

Foot

Round 1: Knit.

Round 2: *K1, kfb; repeat from * to the end of the round—6 stitches per needle, 18 stitches total.

Rounds 3–5: Knit.

Round 6: *K1, k2tog; repeat from * to the end of the round—4 stitches per needle, 12 stitches total.

Round 7: Knit.

Stuff the foot lightly with fiberfill.

Round 8: *K1, k2tog, k1; repeat from * on each needle—3 stitches per needle, 9 stitches total.

Cut the yarn, leaving an 8" (20.5cm) tail. Thread the tail onto a tapestry needle, and then draw the yarn through the stitches remaining on the knitting needles. Cinch into a tight gather. Pull the end to the wrong side and trim.

Work the second leg as for the first, placing it 2 stitches to the left of the center stitch marker.

FINISHING

Weave in any remaining ends.

LAMBKIN LIDS

design by mary lou egan

W hat's better than a swirly hat on a sweet baby? A stitch pattern that looks like it changes each round but doesn't. One round knit, one round a simple repeat—this is mindless knitting at its best, and it looks as though you were following a complex chart. One for baby, one for toddler—this is our new go-to gift for the newcomers in our lives.

DIFFICULTY LEVEL
Mindless

SIZES
Baby (Toddler)

FINISHED MEASUREMENTS
Head circumference: 16½ (18¼)" (42 [46]cm)
Crown depth: 7½ (8¼)" (19 [21]cm)

MATERIALS
1 skein Louet Gems Sport, 100% merino wool, 3½ oz (100g), 225 yd (206m), in #80.2303 Cream (second sample shown in #80.2553 Willow)

1 US size 5 (3.75mm) 16" (40cm) circular needle (adjust needle size as necessary to obtain gauge)
1 set US size 5 (3.75mm) double-pointed needles (adjust needle size as necessary to obtain gauge)
Stitch markers
Tapestry needle

GAUGE AFTER BLOCKING
24 stitches and 28 rows = 4" (10cm) in stockinette stitch

STITCH PATTERN
Worked over a multiple of 11 stitches.
Round 1: *Ssk, k6, yo, k3; repeat from * around.
Round 2: Knit.

PATTERN INSTRUCTIONS

With circular needle, cast on 100 (110) stitches. Join to work in the round, being careful not to twist the stitches. Place a stitch marker for the beginning of the round.

Work 6 rounds in (k1, p1) rib. On the last round, *for Baby size only,* decrease by knitting the last 2 stitches together—99 (110) stitches.

Round 1: *Ssk, k6, yo, k3, repeat from * to end of round.

Round 2: Knit.

Work these 2 rounds 17 (19) more times, for a total of 18 (20) times.

CROWN

Note: Change to double-pointed needles when necessary while decreasing.

Round 1 (decrease): *Sk2p, k5, yo, k3; repeat from * to end of round—90 (100) stitches.

Round 2: Knit.

Round 3 (decrease): Sk2p, k4, yo, k3; repeat from * to end of round—81 (90) stitches.

Round 4: Knit.

Round 5 (decrease): Sk2p, k3, yo, k3; repeat from * to end of round—72 (80) stitches.

Round 6: Knit.

Round 7 (decrease): *Sk2p, k2, yo, k3; repeat from * to end of round—63 (70) stitches.

Round 8: Knit.

Round 9 (decrease): Sk2p, k1, yo, k3; repeat from * to end of round—54 (60) stitches.

Round 10 (decrease): *Ssk, k1, yo, k1, ssk; repeat from * to end of round—45 (50) stitches.

Round 11 (decrease): *Ssk, k1, ssk; repeat from * to end of round—27 (30) stitches.

Round 12 (decrease): Sk2p around—9 (10) stitches.

Cut yarn, leaving an 8" (20.5cm) tail. Thread the tail on the tapestry needle, then draw the yarn through the stitches remaining on the knitting needles. Cinch into a tight gather and firmly secure end. Weave in ends.

no sheep at the shore

WE ARE DEDICATED BEACH KNITTERS. KNITTING IN THE dunes can seem incongruous, but we are here to tell you that there's hardly a better spot to relax with a knitting project than by the sea.

There are a few considerations to shoreline knitting. Fuzzy or heavy yarns can feel sticky at the beach, and that's no fun. We like to work with linen and silk and cotton, the same fibers we want to wear when we find ourselves in need of a cover-up, the perfect use for the Kiawah V-neck or the Pompano Tank. The Searsport Market Bag will hold your local produce at the farm stand or tote your towel, novel, and sunglasses to the pool. And the Short Beach Shawl, named for a favorite hangout of ours, is elegantly bohemian with its fringe and open stitchwork and pairs easily with jeans or a dress. Set up shop with your own beverages with the teeny umbrellas and enjoy!

KIAWAH V-NECK

design by mary lou egan

W e just love a breezy linen sweater to throw on at the beach when the air cools. Gently A-line, Kiawah is a top-down seamless raglan design that looks great on everyone: casual or dressy, loose but not boxy, with subtle details like a rolled neck and eyelet trim. It even has a short-row back hem for a little extra coverage. The light gauge gives the linen yarn a beautiful drape and sheen.

DIFFICULTY LEVEL
Relaxed

SIZES
XS (S, M, L, XL, XXL)

FINISHED MEASUREMENTS
Bust: 34 (36, 40, 44, 48, 52)" (86 [91, 101.5, 112, 122, 132]cm)

MATERIALS
6 (7, 8, 10, 11, 12) skeins Quince & Co. Sparrow, 100% organic linen, 1¾ oz (50g), 168 yd (155m), in 217 Pink Grapefruit

1 US size 5 (3.75mm) 24" (60cm) circular needle (adjust needle size as necessary to obtain gauge)
1 set US size 5 (3.75mm) double-pointed needles or 1 US 5 (3.75mm) 16" (40cm) circular needle for sleeves (adjust needle size as necessary to obtain gauge)
Stitch markers
Scrap yarn
Tapestry needle

GAUGE AFTER BLOCKING
22 stitches and 32 rows = 4" (10cm) in stockinette stitch

PATTERN NOTES
Sweater has approximately 2-4" (5-10cm) of positive ease.
German short rows are used to shape the back hem in this sweater. You may substitute a different short-row method if you wish.
Change to double-pointed needles or a smaller circular needle when working the sleeves to accommodate the decreasing number of stitches.
You may need a second needle size for working in the round, as gauge can change when switching from working flat to working in the round, especially in linen.

PATTERN INSTRUCTIONS

With the 24" (60cm) circular needle, cast on 68 (72, 74, 74, 78, 78) stitches.

Purl 1 row.

Setup row (RS): Kfb, k1, RLI, k1, place marker k1, LLI, k8, RLI, k1, place marker, k1, LLI, k40 (44, 46, 46, 50, 50), RLI, k1, place marker, k1, LLI, k8, RLI, k1, place marker, k1, LLI, k1, kfb–78 (82, 84, 84, 88, 88) stitches.

Note: The stitches on either side of the markers are the raglan line stitches. With right side facing, the stitches before the first marker are the left front as worn, the stitches between the first and second marker are the left sleeve, the stitches between the second and third marker are the back, the stitches between the third and fourth marker are the right sleeve, and the remaining stitches are the right front.

Turn work and purl 1 row.

Row 1 (RS): Kfb, (knit to marker, RLI, k1, slip marker, k1, LLI) 4 times, knit to last stitch in row, kfb.

Row 2 (WS): Purl.

Each section of the sweater has been increased by 2 stitches–7 stitches for each front section, 14 stitches for each sleeve section, 45 (49, 51, 51, 55, 55) stitches for back, 88 (92, 94, 94, 98, 98) stitches total.

Repeat rows 1 and 2 an additional 18 (18, 19, 19, 20, 20) times, for a total of 19 (19, 20, 20, 21, 21) times, ending with a right-side row, ready to begin on wrong-side row. Do not turn work–268 (272, 284, 284, 298, 298) stitches.

JOIN FOR V-NECK

With right side facing, join to work in the round and place a stitch marker for the beginning of the round.

Increase round: (Knit to marker, RLI, k1, slip marker, k1, LLI) 4 times, knit to the end of the round.

Next round: Knit.

Repeat the last 2 rounds an additional 1 (3, 6, 11, 12, 15) times, for a total of 2 (4, 7, 12, 13, 16) times—90 (94, 104, 114, 120, 126) stitches in front, 54 (58, 66, 76, 80, 86) stitches in each sleeve, 86 (94, 104, 114, 122, 128) stitches in back, 284 (304, 340, 380, 402, 426) stitches total.

Knit 14 (16, 12, 4, 2, 0) rounds even.

DIVIDE FOR BODY AND SLEEVES

After the beginning of the round, knit to the first marker. Place stitches between the next 2 markers (left sleeve stitches) on scrap yarn, removing markers. Cast on 6 (6, 6, 8, 12, 16) stitches for left underarm, placing a marker after stitch 3 (3, 3, 4, 6, 8) to mark the center of the underarm, and knit across the back stitches to the next marker. Place the stitches between the next 2 markers (right sleeve stitches) on scrap yarn, removing markers. Cast on 6 (6, 6, 8, 12, 16) stitches for right underarm, placing a marker after stitch 3 (3, 3, 4, 6, 8). Knit across the right front stitches to the end of the round—188 (200, 220, 244, 266, 286) stitches.

BODY

Knit 16 (16, 16, 10, 10, 10) rounds. Increase in the next round and every 16th round, for a total of 6 (6, 6, 8, 8, 8) increase rounds, as follows:

Increase round: Knit to 1 stitch before marker, RLI, k1, slip marker, k1, LLI, knit to 1 stitch before marker, RLI, k1, slip marker, k1, LLI, knit to end of round.

Continue in stockinette stitch, working the increase round every 16 rounds an additional 5 (5, 5, 7, 7, 7) times, for a total of 6 (6, 6, 8, 8, 8) times.

⚠ CONCENTRATION ZONE

After completing the last increase round, work short rows for the back as follows:

Knit to 1 stitch before the right underarm marker, turn, slip 1 stitch with yarn in front, pull yarn firmly over the needle to the back to create a double stitch, purl to 1 stitch before the left underarm marker, turn work.

Slip 1 stitch with yarn in front, pull yarn firmly over needle to the back to create a double stitch, knit to within 4 stitches of gap caused by the last turn (3 stitches before double stitch, plus double stitch that is counted as 1 stitch), turn work.

Continue in this manner, slipping the first stitch with yarn in front then pulling the yarn over to the back to create a double stitch, purl to within 4 stitches of the gap caused by the last turn, turn work. Repeat until a total of 6 turns have been worked on each side for a total of 12 short rows, ending having just turned to the right side of the knitting. Knit to the beginning of the round and then knit 1 more round, knitting the 2 loops of the double stitch together when you encounter them.

Work 4 rounds even.

Eyelet Round

Sizes XS, S, M, and L only: *K2tog, yo, k2; repeat from * to end of round.

Sizes XL and XXL only: *K2tog, yo, k2; repeat from * to last 2 stitches before marker, end k2tog, yo.

Knit 10 rounds even, then continue knitting to the first underarm marker to avoid ending the knitting in the center front of the garment. Bind off loosely. Cut the yarn, leaving a tail long enough to weave in.

SLEEVES

With right side of work facing and using double-pointed needles (or a 16" [40cm] circular needle), begin at the center of either underarm and pick up and knit 3 (3, 3, 4, 6, 8) stitches over the cast-on stitches at the underarm. Put the sleeve stitches onto the needles and knit across them. Pick up and knit 3 (3, 3, 4, 6, 8) stitches over the cast-on stitches at the underarm. Place marker for the beginning of the round—60 (64, 72, 84, 92, 102) stitches.

🕸 CRUISE CONTROL

Knit 8 rounds.

Decrease round: K1, k2tog, knit to last 3 stitches before marker, ssk, k1. Continue in stockinette stitch, working the decrease round every 14 (16, 10, 8, 7, 7) rounds an additional 3 (3, 5, 7, 7, 8) times, for a total of 4 (4, 6, 8, 8, 9) times.

Knit 16 (8, 12, 8, 8, 9) rounds, or 2" (5cm) before desired length.

Eyelet round: *K2tog, yo, k2; repeat from * to end of round.

Knit 12 rounds.

Bind off. Cut the yarn, leaving a tail long enough to weave in.

NECK BAND

Attach yarn at the raglan line at the back of the right sleeve. Pick up and knit 40 (44, 46, 46, 50, 50) stitches across the back, 8 stitches across the left shoulder, 32 (32, 34, 34, 35, 35) stitches along the left front of the V-neck, 32 (32, 34, 34, 35, 35) stitches along the right front of the V-neck, and 8 stitches across the right shoulder—120 (124, 130, 130, 136, 136) stitches.

Join to work in the round. Place a stitch marker for the beginning of the round where yarn was attached. Knit 5 rounds.
Bind off. Cut the yarn, leaving a tail long enough to weave in.

FINISHING

Weave in ends.
Block.

TIP
Linen becomes softer, smoother, and takes on more of its true nature after washing. To ensure correct gauge when working with linen, machine wash and dry your linen swatch, then measure the swatch for accurate gauge. Be sure to check yarn label for special instructions. —MLE

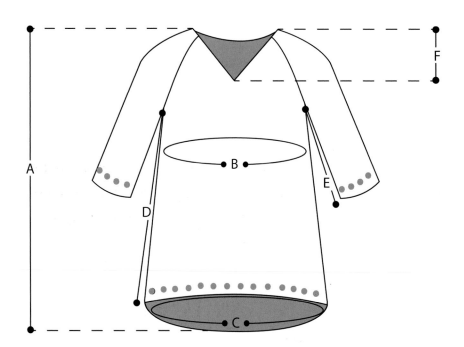

A: 23¼ (24, 24½, 25¾, 26, 26½)" (59 [61, 62, 65, 66, 67]cm)
B: 34 (36, 40, 44, 48, 52)" (87 [92, 101.5, 112.5, 123, 132]cm)
C: 38½ (40½, 44½, 50, 54, 58)" (100 [103.5, 112.5, 127.5, 137.5, 147]cm)
D: 16 (16, 16, 17, 17, 17)" (40.5 [40.5, 40.5, 43, 43, 43]cm)
E: 12 (12, 12, 12, 12, 12)" (30.5 [30.5, 30.5, 30.5, 30.5, 30.5]cm)
F: 7¼ (8, 8½, 8¾, 9, 9½)" (18.75 [20.5, 21.5, 22.5, 23, 24]cm)

POMPANO TANK

design by kirsten kapur

The Pompano Tank is the perfect garment for strolling the beach or grabbing a drink at a boardwalk café. With its breezy A-line shape and playful array of eyelets along the hem, this body-skimming garment will make you feel like skipping at the water's edge.

DIFFICULTY LEVEL
Relaxed

SIZES
XS (S, M, L, 1X, 2X)

FINISHED MEASUREMENTS
Bust: 30½ (34½, 38½, 42½, 46½, 50½)" (77.5 [87.5, 98, 108, 118, 128.5]cm)

MATERIALS
3 (3, 4, 4, 5, 5) skeins Louet Euroflax Sport, 100% linen, 3½ oz (100g), 270 yd (246m), in #2424 Eggplant

1 US size 5 (3.75mm) 24" (60cm) circular needle (adjust needle size as necessary to obtain gauge)
5 stitch markers
Scrap yarn
Tapestry needle

GAUGE AFTER BLOCKING
20 stitches and 30 rows = 4" (10cm) in stockinette stitch

STITCH PATTERN
Eyelet Pattern
  Worked over a multiple of 4 stitches.
  Rounds 1-3: Knit.

Round 4: *Yo, k2tog, k2; repeat from * to end of round.
Rounds 5-7: Knit.
Round 8: *K2, yo, ssk; repeat from * to end of round.
Repeat rounds 1-8 for pattern.

PATTERN NOTE
This tunic is worked in one piece in the round from the bottom up. The front and back are separated at the armholes and worked back and forth from there.

PATTERN INSTRUCTIONS

LOWER EDGE

Cast on 188 (208, 228, 248, 268, 288) stitches.

Join to work in the round, being careful not to twist the stitches.

Place a stitch marker for the beginning of the round.

Purl 1 round.

Work rounds 1-8 of eyelet pattern a total of 6 times. Work rounds 1-4 once more for a total of 52 rows worked in eyelet pattern.

BODY

Setup round: K24 (26, 29, 31, 34, 36), place marker, k46 (52, 56, 62, 66, 72), place marker, k48 (52, 58, 62, 68, 72), place marker, k46 (52, 56, 62, 66, 72), place marker, k24 (26, 29, 31, 34, 36).

Round 1 (decrease): Slip beginning-of-round marker, knit to 2 stitches before next marker, k2tog, slip marker, knit to next marker, slip marker, ssk, knit to 2 stitches before next marker, k2tog, slip marker, knit to next marker, slip marker, ssk, knit to end–184 (204, 224, 244, 264, 284) stitches.

Rounds 2-7: Knit.

Work these 7 rounds 8 more times, for a total of 9 times–152 (172, 192, 212, 232, 252) stitches.

Remove shaping markers on the last decrease round, keeping only the beginning-of-round marker in place.

Work in stockinette stitch until piece measures 18 (18, 17¾, 17½, 17¼, 17)" (45.5 [45.5, 45, 44.5, 44, 43]cm) from the cast-on edge.

SEPARATE FRONT AND BACK

Knit to the last 6 (8, 8, 10, 10, 12) stitches.

Continuing in the round, bind off the next 12 (16, 16, 20, 20, 24) stitches, removing the beginning-of-round marker when you get to it.

Knit 63 (69, 79, 85, 95, 101) stitches.

Place these 64 (70, 80, 86, 96, 102) stitches (the stitches just knit and the stitch left from the bind-off) on a piece of scrap yarn.

Bind off the next 12 (16, 16, 20, 20, 24) stitches, knit to the end–64 (70, 80, 86, 96, 102) stitches remain (the stitches just knit and the stitch left from the bind-off).

Turn work.

BACK

Shape Armhole

Row 1 (WS): Purl.

Row 2 (decrease) (RS): K1, ssk, knit to last 3 stitches, k2tog, k1–62 (68, 78, 84, 94, 100) stitches.

Repeat the last 2 rows 2 (2, 4, 4, 8, 8) more times, for a total of 3 (3, 5, 5, 9, 9) times–58 (64, 70, 76, 78, 84) stitches.

Continue in stockinette stitch until armhole measures 6½ (7, 7½, 8, 8½, 9)" (16.5 [18, 19, 20.5, 21.5, 23]cm). End with a wrong-side row, ready to begin a right-side row.

Shape Back Neck and Shoulders

Knit 14 (17, 18, 20, 19, 21) stitches and place them on a piece of scrap yarn.

Bind off the next 30 (30, 34, 36, 40, 42) stitches, k13 (16, 17, 19, 18, 20)–14 (17, 18, 20, 19, 21) stitches remain (the stitches just knit and the stitch left from the bind-off).

Turn work.

Back Left Shoulder

Row 1 (WS): Purl.

Row 2 (decrease) (RS): K1, ssk, k7 (9, 9, 11, 10, 11), wrap the next stitch and turn (see Techniques, page 138).

Row 3: Purl.

Row 4 (decrease): K1, ssk, k2 (3, 3, 4, 4, 4), wrap the next stitch and turn.

Row 5: Purl.

Row 6 (decrease): K1, ssk, knit to end, picking up the wraps and knitting them together with the wrapped stitch as you come to them–11 (14, 15, 17, 16, 18) stitches.

Bind off.

Back Right Shoulder

Place the 14 (17, 18, 20, 19, 21) held shoulder stitches on the needle. With wrong side facing, rejoin yarn at right neck edge.

Row 1 (WS): Purl.

Row 2 (decrease) (RS): Knit to last 3 stitches, k2tog, k1.

Row 3: P9 (11, 11, 13, 12, 13), wrap the next stitch and turn.

Row 4 (decrease): Knit to last 3 stitches, k2tog, k1.

Row 5: P4 (5, 5, 6, 6, 6), wrap the next stitch and turn.

Row 6 (decrease): Knit to last 3 stitches, k2tog, k1.

Row 7: Purl, picking up the wraps and purling them together with the stitch as you come to them–11 (14, 15, 17, 16, 18) stitches.

Bind off.

FRONT

Place the held 64 (70, 80, 86, 96, 102) front stitches on the needle. With wrong side facing, rejoin the yarn at the right armhole edge. Work as for back until armhole measures 3½ (4, 4, 4½, 5, 5)" (9 [10, 10, 11.5, 12.5, 12.5]cm). End with a wrong-side row, ready to begin a right-side row.

Shape Front Neck

Knit 16 (19, 20, 22, 21, 23) stitches and place them on a piece of scrap yarn.

Bind off the next 26 (26, 30, 32, 36, 38) stitches, k15 (18, 19, 21, 20, 22)−16 (19, 20, 22, 21, 23) stitches remain (the stitches just knit and the stitch left from the bind-off). Turn work.

Right Front

Row 1 (WS): Purl.

Row 2 (decrease) (RS): K1, ssk, knit to end−15 (18, 19, 21, 20, 22) stitches. Repeat the last 2 rows 4 more times, for a total of 5 times−11 (14, 15, 17, 16, 18) stitches.

Continue to work in stockinette stitch until the armhole measures 6½ (7, 7½, 8, 8½, 9)" (16.5 [18, 19, 20.5, 21.5, 23]cm). End with a right-side row, ready to begin a wrong-side row.

Right Shoulder

Row 1 (WS): Purl.

Row 2 (RS): K7 (9, 9, 11, 10, 11), wrap the next stitch and turn.

Row 3: Purl.

Row 4: K3 (4, 4, 5, 5, 5), wrap the next stitch and turn.

Row 5: Purl.

Row 6: Knit to end, picking up the wraps and knitting them together with the stitch as you come to them.
Bind off.

Left Front

Place the 16 (19, 20, 22, 21, 23) held stitches on the needle. With the wrong side facing, rejoin the yarn.

Row 1 (WS): Purl.

Row 2 (decrease) (RS): Knit to last 3 stitches, k2tog, k1−15 (18, 19, 21, 20, 22) stitches.
Repeat the last 2 rows 4 more times, for a total of 5 times−11 (14, 15, 17, 16, 18) stitches.

Continue to work in stockinette stitch until the armhole measures 6½ (7, 7½, 8, 8½, 9)" (16.5 [18, 19, 20.5, 21.5, 23]cm). End with a right-side row, ready to begin a wrong-side row.

Row 1 (WS): Purl.

Row 2 (RS): Knit.

Row 3: P7 (9, 9, 11, 10, 11), wrap the next stitch and turn.

Row 4: Knit.

Row 5: P3 (4, 4, 5, 5, 5), wrap the next stitch and turn.

Row 6: Knit.

Row 7: Purl, picking up the wraps and purling them together with the stitch as you come to them.
Bind off.

FINISHING

Sew front to back at shoulder seams.
Weave in ends.
Block to measurements in schematic.

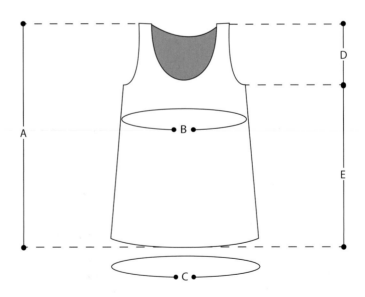

A: 24½ (25, 25¼, 25½, 25¾, 26)" (62 [63.5, 64, 65, 65.5, 66]cm)
B: 30½ (34½, 28½, 42½, 46½, 50½)" (77.5 [87.5, 98, 108, 118, 128.5]cm)
C: 37½ (41½, 45½, 49½, 53½, 57½)" (95.5 [105.5, 115.5, 125.5, 136, 146]cm)
D: 6½ (7, 7½, 8, 8½, 9)" (16.5 [18, 19, 20.5, 21.5, 23]cm)
E: 18 (18, 17¾, 17½, 17¼, 17)" (45.5 [45.5, 45, 44.5, 44, 43]cm)

SHORT BEACH SHAWL

design by kirsten kapur

The Short Beach Shawl is the project you imagine yourself knitting happily on the beach, watching the waves roll in and out. When evening comes and your friends and family want to head back to the house, you won't want to put it down. Worked at a loose gauge for maximum drape, the finished shawl is perfect for tossing over your shoulders on cool evenings, or for wearing sarong-style over your bathing suit. The fringe adds to the lighthearted, bohemian flair of this classic summer accessory.

DIFFICULTY LEVEL
Relaxed

SIZES
S (M, L)
Shown in size M

FINISHED MEASUREMENTS
Approximate width: 62½ (68, 73½)"
(159 [172.5, 186.5]cm) across top edge
Approximate length: 25 (28, 31)" (63.5
[71, 79]cm) from top edge to point,
excluding fringe

MATERIALS
2 (2, 2) skeins Dragonfly Fibers Dance
Rustic Silk, 100% silk noil, 4 oz (113.5g),
450 yd (411.5m), in Titania

1 pair US size 8 (5mm) straight needles
(adjust needle size as necessary to
obtain gauge)

Tapestry needle
US size G-6 (4mm) crochet hook

GAUGE AFTER BLOCKING
13 stitches and 25 rows = 4" (10cm) in
garter stitch

STITCH PATTERN
Flowers
Every right-side row of the flowers
pattern increases the overall stitch
count by 2 stitches. The pattern repeat
is between the *'s and is a multiple of
6 stitches.
Row 1 (RS): K2, yo, k1, *yo, sk2p, yo,
k3; repeat from * to last 6 stitches, yo,
sk2p, yo, k1, yo, k2.
Row 2 and all wrong side rows through
row 6: Knit.
Row 3: K2, yo, k2tog, yo, *k3, yo, sk2p,
yo; repeat from * to last 7 stitches, k3,
yo, ssk, yo, k2.

Row 5: K2, yo, k3, *yo, sk2p, yo, k3;
repeat from * to last 8 stitches, yo,
sk2p, yo, k3, yo, k2.
Repeat rows 1–6 for pattern.

PATTERN NOTES
This shawl is worked in one piece
beginning from the bottom point and
increasing upward to the top edge.
The stated gauge is approximate. The
nature of this fabric is to stretch, and
gauge will vary with how the piece is
blocked.
The overall stitch count increases by
2 stitches on every right-side row.
The fringe is optional. Without fringe,
the yarn requirements will be 1 (1, 2)
skeins.

PATTERN INSTRUCTIONS

SETUP
Cast on 5 stitches.
Row 1 and all wrong-side rows through row 11: Knit.
Row 2 (increase) (RS): K2, yo, k1, yo, k2–7 stitches.
Row 4 (increase): K2, yo, k3, yo, k2–9 stitches.
Row 6 (increase): K2, yo, k1, yo, sk2p, yo, k1, yo, k2–11 stitches.
Row 8 (increase): K2, yo, k2tog, yo, k3, yo, ssk, yo, k2–13 stitches.
Row 10 (increase): K2, yo, k3, yo, sk2p, yo, k3, yo, k2–15 stitches.

BODY OF SHAWL
Row 1 and all right-side rows through row 11 (increase): K2, yo, knit to last 2 stitches, yo, k2.
Row 2 and all wrong-side rows through row 12: Knit–27 stitches after row 12.
Rows 13-18: Work flowers pattern–33 stitches after row 18.
Work rows 1-18 above 7 (8, 9) more times, for a total of 8 (9, 10) times–159 (177, 195) stitches.
Work rows 1-12 only once more–171 (189, 207) stitches.

Top Edge
Row 1 (increase) (RS): K2, yo, k1, (yo, k2tog) to last 2 stitches, yo, k2–173 (191, 209) stitches.
Row 2 (WS): Knit.
Row 3 (increase): K2, yo, knit to last 2 stitches, yo, k2–175 (193, 211) stitches.
Row 4: Knit.
Bind off very loosely.

FINISHING
Weave in ends.
Block.

Fringe
The fringe is inserted through the eyelets along the 2 sides of the shawl. Do not fringe the top edge.
Cut 680 (752, 824) 11" (28cm) strands of yarn.
Insert the crochet hook into the first eyelet on the right side of the shawl, from front to back.
Take 4 yarn strands and hold them together with the ends neatly aligned.
Fold the 4 strands in half and put the folded end over the crochet hook.
Using the crochet hook pull the folded end about halfway through the eyelet from the wrong side to the right side.
Bring the cut ends through the folded end and tighten to secure.
Continue with each eyelet along both sides of the shawl.
Trim ends evenly when finished.

TIP
When making fringe, I try to find a book that has a circumference close to my desired fringe length—paperbacks work well for this. I wrap the yarn around the book, once for each piece of fringe. Once the yarn has been wrapped the required number of times, I slip the yarn from the book, being careful to keep all of the loops together and even. Finally, I cut the loops to create my pieces of fringe, all of equal length. —KAGK

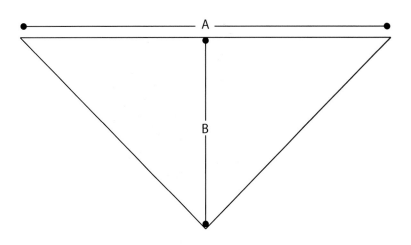

A: 62½ (68, 73½)" (159 [173, 186.5]cm)
B: 25 (28, 31)" (63.5 [71, 79]cm)

SEARSPORT MARKET BAG

design by mary lou egan

Whether you need a bag for the beach, the market, or your knitting itself, this versatile and stretchy sack has you covered. The market bag replaces plastic bags, and with yarn made from recycled jeans it's "green," too. This easy-to-memorize pattern is perfect for beach knitting—every other round is the same simple repeat, with a purl round in between. The strap is knotted to make it easily adjustable.

DIFFICULTY LEVEL
Relaxed

SIZE
One size

FINISHED MEASUREMENTS
21½" (57cm) circumference and 12" (30.48cm) from cast-on edge.

MATERIALS
3 skeins Berroco Indigo, 95% recycled cotton, 5% other fibers, 3½ oz (100g), 219 yd (200m), in #6410 Relaxed

1 US size 7 (4.5mm) 24" (60cm) circular needle (adjust needle size as necessary to obtain gauge)
Stitch markers
Tapestry needle

GAUGE AFTER BLOCKING
20 stitches and 28 rows = 4" (10cm) in stockinette stitch
18 stitches and 26 rows = 4" (10cm) in ripple stitch

STITCH PATTERN
Ripple Stitch (worked over 14 stitches)
  Round 1: *K2, yo, k3, ssk, k2tog, k3, yo, k2; repeat from * around.
  Round 2: Purl.
  Repeat rounds 1 and 2 for pattern.

PATTERN INSTRUCTIONS

Cast on 70 stitches.

Row 1 (RS): Knit.

Row 2 (WS): Purl.

Work these 2 rows for a total of 43 rows, ending just having worked a right-side row.

With right side of work facing, turn the piece clockwise 90° so that the cast-on edge is now at the left, and pick up and knit 42 stitches along the short side of the rectangle. Turn clockwise so that the cast-on edge is at the top. Pick up and knit 70 stitches along this edge. Turn clockwise one more time and pick up and knit 42 stitches along the other short side of the rectangle—224 stitches.

Place marker for the beginning of the round.

Knit 24 rounds.

Work rounds 1 and 2 of ripple stitch 24 times (48 rounds), or until 7½" (19cm) from beginning of ripple stitch or to desired length.

EDGE

Round 1: *K2, yo, k3, ssk, k2tog, k3, yo, k2; repeat from * to end of round.

Round 2: Knit.

Work edge rounds 1 and 2 twice more, for a total of 6 edge rounds.

DRAWSTRING HOLE ROUNDS

Round 1: *K3, ssk, k2tog, yo twice, ssk, k2tog, k3; repeat from * to end of round.

Round 2: *K5, k1, p1 in double yo, k5; repeat from * to end of round. Work 5 rounds even. Bind off.

DRAWSTRING/STRAP

Cast on 6 stitches. Knit every row until piece measures 60" (152.5cm). Bind off, leaving an end long enough to weave in.

FINISHING

Beginning at center front, thread the drawstring/strap through the holes made by the double yarn overs. Weave in ends. Knot the ends of the strap together.
Weave in ends.

TIP

Mindless knitting sometimes needs an assist. In addition to the beginning-of-the-round stitch marker, add one marker between each of the repeats until the pattern is clear. This also helps you identify mistakes more easily. Instead of searching the entire round, use the markers to break it down into smaller, more manageable sections for your detective work. —MLE

difficulty ratings

Each pattern in this book is rated in terms of concentration required so you can better choose projects to suit whatever situation you're in.

Mindless—These are the simplest projects, patterns that can be knit in a bar or while hanging out with your rowdiest knitting friends. They are mostly stockinette or garter stitch with simple increases and decreases.

Relaxed—These projects can be done out of the corner of your eye, while watching a movie or enjoying conversation with a friend. You might need to pay attention now and then. They include simple cables or lace patterns so you can focus on other things.

Attentive—These projects, while still not extremely difficult, will occasionally require a little focus and attention to detail. Involving more complex cables, lace, and attached borders, they take a bit of knitting know-how.

abbreviations and definitions

cdd–central double decrease
Slip 2 stitches together knitwise; knit the next stitch; pass the 2 slipped stitches together over the knit stitch.

k–knit

k2tog–knit 2 stitches together

kfb–knit into the front and back
Knit into the front of the stitch without removing it from the needle, then knit into the back leg of the same stitch, creating an extra stitch.

LLI–left-leaning lifted increase
With left needle, lift the left leg of the stitch below the last knitted stitch onto the needle and knit this stitch.

RLI–right-leaning lifted increase
With right needle, lift the right leg of the stitch below the next stitch onto the left needle and knit this stitch.

M1L–make 1 left
Using the tip of the left needle, pick up the bar between the stitches from front to back and knit it though the back loop.

M1R–make 1 right
Using the tip of the left needle, pick up the bar between the stitches from back to front and knit it though the front loop.

p–purl

sk2p–slip 1, knit 2 together, pass slipped stitch over
Slip the first stitch on the left needle knitwise, knit the the next 2 stitches together, pass the slipped stitch over the 2 knit together.

ssk–slip, slip, knit
Slip the first stitch on the left needle knitwise, slip the next stitch on the left needle knitwise, knit these 2 stitches together.

tbl–through back loop
Work the stitch through the leg of the loop that is on the back side of the needle.

slip wyib–slip 1 stitch purlwise from the left needle to the right needle, with yarn in back

slip wyif–slip 1 stitch purlwise from the left needle to the right needle, with yarn in front

yo–yarn over
Wrap the yarn around the right needle, and bring it back into position to work the next stitch.

techniques

WRAP AND TURN

On a knit row: Work to the stitch to be wrapped, move the yarn to the front of the work, slip the stitch to be wrapped onto the right needle purlwise. Move the yarn to the back of the work. Slip the stitch to be wrapped back onto the left needle. Turn work.

On a purl row: Work to the stitch to be wrapped, move the yarn to the back of the work, slip the stitch to be wrapped onto the right needle purlwise. Move the yarn to the front of the work. Slip the stitch to be wrapped back onto the left needle. Turn work.

NOTES ON SIZING SOCKS

The length of the feet of the sock designs in this book is customizable, therefore it is not necessary to select a size based on foot length. Instead, select your size based on the desired finished circumference. Since socks should be worn with 1-2" of negative ease, you should select a size where the circumference is 1-2" less than the widest part of the foot. To customize the foot length, follow the instructions in the patterns. You will be instructed to work the foot length, less the length of the toe.

PURLED BIND-OFF

Step 1: Purl the first stitch.

Step 2: Purl the next stitch.

Step 3: Pass the first stitch purled over the second stitch.

Repeat steps 2 and 3 until all stitches have been bound off.

THREE-NEEDLE BIND-OFF

Setup: Hold the two needles with the live stitches parallel to each other in your left hand.

Step 1: Knit the first stitch from each needle together with a third needle.

Step 2: Knit the next stitch from each needle together.

Step 3: Pass the first stitch knit over the second stitch.

Repeat steps 2 and 3 until all stitches have been bound off.

K1, P1 BIND-OFF

Cut the yarn, leaving a tail three times the length of the knitting to be bound off, and thread the tail onto a tapestry needle.

Step 1: Insert the tapestry needle into the first knit stitch knitwise and slip this stitch off the knitting needle. Pull the yarn through.

Step 2: Skip the first purl stitch by bringing the tapestry needle in front of the purl stitch. Insert the tapestry needle purlwise into the next knit stitch and pull the yarn through.

Step 3: Insert the tapestry needle into the first purl stitch purlwise and slip this stitch off the knitting needle. Pull the yarn through.

Step 4: Skip the next knit stitch by bringing the tapestry needle behind the knit stitch. Insert the tapestry needle knitwise into the back leg of the next purl stitch and pull the yarn through.

Repeat steps 1-4 until one stitch remains, insert the tapestry needle purlwise through this stitch, draw the yarn through and secure end.

KITCHENER STITCH

Thread a blunt tapestry needle with the tail of yarn. Hold the two knitting needles parallel.

Step 1: Insert tapestry needle into first stitch of front needle as if to knit and slip the stitch off.

Step 2: Insert tapestry needle into second stitch of front needle as if to purl, leaving the stitch on the knitting needle, and draw the yarn through.

Step 3: Insert tapestry needle into first stitch of back needle as if to purl and slip the stitch off.

Step 4: Insert tapestry needle into second stitch of back needle as if to knit, leaving the stitch on the knitting needle, and draw the yarn through.

Repeat these 4 steps until all stitches are woven together.

yarn sources

~~~~~~~~

We are deeply indebted to the following companies who provided yarn support for the patterns in this book.

Anzula Luxury Fibers
www.anzula.com

Berroco
www.berroco.com

Briggs & Little
www.briggsandlittle.com

Classic Elite Yarns
www.classiceliteyarns.com

Dragonfly Fibers
www.dragonflyfibers.com

Fibre Company
www.thefibreco.com

Lion Brand Yarn
www.lionbrand.com

Louet North America
www.louet.com

Malabrigo
www.malabrigoyarn.com

Neighborhood Fiber Company
www.neighborhoodfiberco.com

Plymouth Yarn Company
www.plymouthyarn.com

Quince & Co.
www.quinceandco.com

Rowan
www.knitrowan.com

Swans Island
www.swansislandcompany.com

Zen Yarn Garden
www.zenyarngarden.co

alternate yarn suggestions by pattern

Abide Shawl
Malabrigo Sock
Anzula Cloud
Stonehedge Fiber Mill Shepherd's
Wool Fine

Apple Hill Finger Puppets
Brown Sheep Nature Spun Sport
Plymouth Galway Sport

Bambino Blanket
HiKoo Sueño Worsted
Neighborhood Fiber Co. Studio
Worsted
Louet Gems Worsted

Bear in a Bunny Suit
Berroco Ultra Alpaca
Classic Elite Mountain Top Vista
Fibre Company Knightsbridge

Camurac Cardigan
Lion Brand Fisherman's Wool
Briggs & Little Heritage
Madelinetosh Tosh Chunky

Galworthy Gift Bag
Hand Maiden Fine Yarn Swiss Silk
Louisa Harding Amitola
Shibui Knits Pebble

Glama Wrap
Rowan Cocoon
The Fibre Company Tundra
Misti Alpaca Tonos Chunky

Grand Central Scarf
Lion Brand LB Collection Superwash
Merino
Shalimar Yarns Breathless DK
Plymouth DK Merino Superwash

Headford Hat
Berroco Artisan
Schoppel Reggae

Idlewild Socks
Hand Maiden Fine Yarn Casbah Sock
Dream in Color Smooshy with
Cashmere
Dragonfly Fibers Djinni Sock

Joggle Scarf
Plymouth Gina
Skacel Reggae Ombre
Noro Kuryeon

Keynote Pullover
Classic Elite Soft Linen
Neighborhood Fiber Co. Studio DK

Kiawah V-neck
Shibui Knits Linen
Louet Euroflax Sport

Lambkin Lids
Classic Elite Liberty Wool Light
HiKoo Sueño

Lucy and Ethel Cowl
Berroco Ultra Alpaca
Classic Elite Mountain Top Vista
Quince & Co. Owl

Maplewood Pillow
Plymouth Galway Worsted
Berroco Vintage
Brown Sheep Nature Spun Worsted

Oxbo Socks
Briggs & Little Regal
Lion Brand Wool-Ease

Parley Cardigan
Classic Elite Song
Neighborhood Fiber Co. Studio DK

Polliwog Popover
Classic Elite Liberty Wool Light
Milla Mia Naturally Soft Merino
HiKoo Sueño

Pompano Tank
Quince & Co. Sparrow
Rowan Cotton Glace
Classic Elite Yarns Firefly

Portillo Cowl
Rowan Big Wool
Plymouth De Aire
Classic Elite Yarns Toboggan

Searsport Market Bag
Knit One Crochet Too 2nd Time
Cotton
Lion Brand Cotton-Ease
Tahki Cotton Classic

Shandy Headband
Madelinetosh Tosh DK
Plymouth DK Merino Superwash
Dream in Color Everlasting DK

Sharline Boot Toppers
Brown Sheep Lambs Pride Worsted
Quince & Co. Osprey
Briggs & Little Heritage

Short Beach Shawl
Shibui Knits Linen
Bergere de France Soie
Manos Del Uruguay Fino

Sidekick Hat
Quince & Co. Chickadee
Brooklyn Tweed Loft
HiKoo Llamor

Star-Eyed Julep Throw
Plymouth Galway Worsted
Berroco Vintage
Brown Sheep Nature Spun Worsted

Turoa Mitts
Blue Sky Alpacas Alpaca Silk
Berroco Ultra Alpaca Light
Classic Elite Fresco

Westerloe Dog Sweater
Plymouth Encore
Lion Brand Cotton-Ease
Berroco Vintage

acknowledgments

This book was born of our love of knitting together. By that, we mean the literal connecting of stitches as well as the joy of making in one another's company. As we schemed and dreamed and designed and knit and laughed and joked and knit some more, we were joined by designers, assistants, friends, family, and so many talented souls who generously contributed to make this book happen.

We're thankful especially for the indispensable work of our technical editor, Ellen Silva, who meticulously went over patterns and instructions with dedication, expertise, and a fabulous sense of humor.

We would like to thank the following people, companies, and shops who helped us during research and production of this book, starting with Caitlin Harpin, formerly of Potter Craft, and Rebecca Davison of Ravenmark, Inc., who cheered us on from the start.

Emma Brodie, our ultimate editor, for jumping in enthusiastically, encouraging us to be ourselves, and making four-hour meetings painless. We would also like to thank the rest of our team at Potter, including Debbie Glasserman for her beautiful book design, Stephanie Huntwork, Patricia Shaw, Phil Leung, Doris Cooper, and Aaron Wehner.

Our guest contributing designers: Susan B. Anderson, Kay Gardiner and Ann Shayne of Mason-Dixon Knitting, and Theresa Gaffey said yes unconditionally and gave us beautiful patterns.

Test knitters: Colleen Abbot, David Anthony, Beverly Army-Williams, Angela Berger, Maddy Brown, La'Ketta Casey, Theresa Gaffey, Ann Holt, Peter Kennedy, Beverly Mazzarella, Lynn Collins McElin, Kari Mink, Devjani Mishra, Linda Reis, Louise Robert-Brunet, Yvonne Spencer, Marilyn Tierney, Robin Turner, Melissa Winders, Anna Wukich, Linda Young.

Models: Josephine Ankrah, Gabe Engler-Zucker, Zoe Engler-Zucker, Madeline Hunter, Sofia Kapur, Katrina Nill, Cassidy Ann Warner, and Dorie the Schnauzer. All lent their heads, hearts, smiles, beauty, and/or feet to show off the knits.

Location and props: Much appreciation to Sandra and David Chen for sharing their beautiful home with us.

Production: Special thanks to Yliana Tibitoski for being an über assistant on photo shoot days and a cheerful helper on tasks ranging from making pompoms to loading cars. Thanks also to Beverly Army Williams for pompom support and to Sarah Walker, who gave us clean, graphic schematics. Karen Clark deserves special recognition for her expert sample knitting and valued input. Last, thanks to Joan Tapper for encouraging words.

Yarn: We're indebted to Jackie Ottino Graf for her amazing color sense and Allison Green for going above and beyond. Please see our yarn source page for complete listings of all those we thank for materials support.

Styling: Raquel Vidal.

Hair and makeup: Deanna D.D. Nickel.

Shops: Knit New Haven in New Haven, Connecticut; Natural Stitches in Pittsburgh, Pennsylvania; Trillium Yarns in Morristown, New Jersey; and the Yarnery in St. Paul, Minnesota.

Last, but definitely not least, we thank Kiran, Guy, and Dave, and all of our families for living the dream, stitch by stitch, along with us.

KAGK, MLE, and GZ, 2016

index